MW00609969

Raising

'Children of the Cross'

(the Spiritual Formation of Children)

Mary Elizabeth Anne Kloska, Fiat. +

En Route Books and Media, LLC
Saint Louis, MO

✠ENROUTE
Make the time

Cover credit: Mary Kloska

Copyright © 2021 Mary Kloska

ISBN- 13: 978-1-956715-07-1

Library of Congress Control Number: 2021950150

I dedicate and consecrate this book to the Infant Weeping Heart of Jesus – with all of His wounds, and all of His Love. Fiat. +

Table of Contents

Chapter 1

Introduction

"Be who God made you to be and you will set the world on fire!"

- Catherine of Siena

"The only tragedy in life is not to become a saint."

- Leon Bloy

"I wish to be a saint...I demand that you be saints. Sanctity is not a luxury, but it is an obligation. And it is not difficult."

- St. Maximillian Kolbe

I cannot think of better quotes to open a book about the spiritual formation of children. Each human soul is knitted together in his or her mother's womb and given the breath of life for one single purpose: to be who God created him or her to be (the *saint* that God created him or her to be) by knowing Him, loving Him, and serving Him (doing His will) here on earth and then forever in eternity. This is the purpose of this book - to help the reader in the formation of children so that they grow up to do just this. By 'being who God made us to be,' we set the world on fire (with His Love) - we change it forever - and we conform ourselves to be more and more like Him.

At the beginning of time when God made Adam and Eve (and at the beginning of *our* time when God knit each one of us individually in our mother's womb), we were created 'in the image and likeness of God.' Both original sin and actual sin warped this image – and so through the Sacraments, by growing in holiness and becoming who God truly created us to be, we grow in conformity to Him (and thus we grow in union with Him).

This is the point of life.

The instrument that God gave to us to use in this formation and transformation of the human soul is the Cross. The Cross was the greatest sermon Jesus ever gave – He preached by example, through suffering, in Love. From the Cross come the Sacraments. On the Cross, we see all wounds healed, all sins forgiven, all division united, all darkness enlightened, all fears quelled, all suffering comforted. The more we conform ourselves to Jesus crucified, the more we are resurrected one with Him.

And so that is the job of anyone in charge of forming children – to teach them about Jesus' love on the Cross, to help them conform themselves in virtue to Jesus according and unto the Cross and to show them the joy of the Resurrection even in the midst of the Cross.

St. Louis de Montfort so beautifully describes this point of life in his letter to the 'Friends of the Cross'. Here he outlines the whole goal of our lives – and his words can be used as a model when we meditate on how God is asking us to form the children He entrusts to us. St. Louis writes:

"Our loving Savior's group is to the right, scaling a narrow path made all the narrower by the world's corruption. Our kind Master is in the lead, barefooted, thorn-crowned, robed in His Blood and weighted with

a heavy Cross. There is only a handful of people who follow Him, but they are the bravest of the brave. His gentle voice is not heard above the tumult of the world, or men do not have the courage to follow Him in poverty, suffering, humiliation and in the other crosses His servants must bear all the days of their life.... To the right, the little flock that follows Jesus can speak only of tears, penance, prayer and contempt for worldly things. Sobbing in their grief, they can be heard repeating: 'Let us suffer, let us weep, let us fast, let us pray, let us hide, let us humble ourselves, let us be poor, let us mortify ourselves, for he who has not the spirit of Christ, the spirit of the Cross, is none of Christ's. Those who are Christ's have crucified their flesh with its concupiscence. We must be conformed to the image of Jesus Christ or else be damned!' 'Be brave,' they keep saying to each other, 'be brave, for if God is for us, in us and leading us, who dare be against us? The One Who is dwelling within us is stronger than the one who is in the world; no servant is above his master; one moment of light tribulation worketh an eternal weight of glory; there are fewer elect than man may think; only the brave and daring take Heaven by storm; the crown is given only to those who strive lawfully according to the Gospel, not according to the fashion of the world. Let us put all our strength into the fight, and run very fast to reach the goal and win the crown.' Friends of the Cross spur each other on with such Divine words."

The natural purity of a child's heart enables him or her to quickly enter into Jesus' Heart Crucified and be molded into the form of His Love. And Jesus' Love molds us ultimately into the saints we were created to be. For this reason, if a child is surrounded by holiness and good formation from the smallest of age, he or she will absorb it as a sponge and become a powerful tool in changing the world. We see this in the words of St. Pope John Paul II to children, written in 1994:

From Pope John Paul II's *Letter to Children* published December 13, 1994:

"...Jesus and his Mother often choose children and give them important tasks for the life of the Church and of humanity...The Redeemer of humanity seems to share with them his concern for others: for parents, for other boys and girls. He eagerly awaits their prayers. **What enormous power the prayer of children has!** This becomes a model for grown-ups themselves: praying with simple and complete trust means praying as children pray...

And here I come to an important point in this Letter: at the end of this Year of the Family, dear young friends, **it is to your prayers that I want to entrust the problems of your own families, and of all the families in the world.** And not only this: I also have other intentions to ask you to pray for. The Pope counts very much on your prayers. We must pray together and pray hard, that humanity, made up of billions of human beings, may become more and more the family of God and able to live in peace. At the beginning of this Letter I mentioned the unspeakable suffering which many children have experienced in this century, and which many of them are continuing to endure at this very moment. How many of them, even in these days, are becoming victims of the hatred which is raging in different parts of the world: in the Balkans, for example, and in some African countries. It was while I was thinking about these facts, which fill our hearts with pain, that **I decided to ask you, dear boys and girls, to take upon yourselves the duty of praying for peace.** You know this well: love and harmony build peace, hatred and violence destroy it. You instinctively turn away from hatred and are attracted by love: for this reason the Pope is certain that you will not refuse his request, but that you will join in his prayer for peace in the world with the same enthusiasm with which you pray for peace and harmony in your own families..."

Imagine that! A Pope that entrusts the most painful, difficult, and sorrowful situations in the world to the **_prayer of children_**!

That is exactly what I – following his footsteps – intend to do as well.

Why does he do this? It's very simple. Simply for the sake of love… in their purity of heart and open-hearted goodness, children are most powerful instruments of Divine Grace to reach others in the world. And because of their simple trust and natural tendency towards selfless love, they find in their littleness (which spontaneously trusts in the Father's Goodness) a courage to face the Cross with courage and faithfulness.

The weapon that a childlike heart has which conquers even the Heart of God is that of true authentic Love. And that is why Jesus taught:

"For the one who is least among all of you is the one who is the greatest." (Lk (:48)

And

"You must become like a little child to enter the Kingdom of Heaven." (Mt 18:3)

Section One

Models for Children

Baby Jesus

The Infant Mary

Children in Scripture

Children Who Are Saints

Chapter 2

Baby Jesus

The greatest Child in all of Scripture is Baby Jesus, the Son of God. We first meet Him in the prophesies:

> *"For a child is born to us, a son is given to us;*
> *upon his shoulder dominion rests.*
> *They name him Wonder-Counselor, God-Hero,*
> *Father-Forever, Prince of Peace."*
>
> - Isaiah 9:5

Then we meet Him in the Annunciation:

> *"In the sixth month, the angel Gabriel was sent from God to a town of Galilee called Nazareth, to a virgin betrothed to a man named Joseph, of the house of David, and the virgin's name was Mary. And coming to her, he said, "Hail, favored one! The Lord is with you." But she was greatly troubled at what was said and pondered what sort of greeting this might be. Then the angel said to her, "Do not be afraid, Mary, for you have found favor with God. Behold, you will conceive in your womb and bear a son, and you shall name him Jesus. He will be great and will be called Son of the Most High, and the Lord God will give him the throne of David his father, and he will rule over the house of Jacob forever, and of his kingdom there will be no end." But Mary said to the angel, "How can this be,*

since I have no relations with a man?" And the angel said to her in reply, "The Holy Spirit will come upon you, and the power of the Most High will overshadow you. Therefore the child to be born will be called holy, the Son of God. And behold, Elizabeth, your relative, has also conceived a son in her old age, and this is the sixth month for her who was called barren; for nothing will be impossible for God." Mary said, "Behold, I am the handmaid of the Lord. May it be done to me according to your word." Then the angel departed from her." –

Matthew 1:26-38

We hear about Him in St. Joseph's dream:

"When his mother Mary was betrothed to Joseph, but before they lived together, she was found with child through the Holy Spirit. Joseph her husband, since he was a righteous man, yet unwilling to expose her to shame, decided to divorce her quietly.

Such was his intention when, behold, the angel of the Lord appeared to him in a dream and said, "Joseph, son of David, do not be afraid to take Mary your wife into your home. <u>For it is through the Holy Spirit that this child has been conceived</u> in her. <u>She will</u>

bear a son and you are to name him Jesus, because he
will save his people from their sins."

All this took place to fulfill what the Lord had said
through the prophet: "Behold, the virgin shall be with
child and bear a son, and they shall name him
Emmanuel," which means "God is with us." –

Matthew 1:18-23

We see the great power of Baby Jesus – still hidden as a tiny Embryo within His Mother's womb – in the story of the Visitation. It is through the presence of Baby Jesus within Mary that John the Baptist is baptized by the Holy Spirit:

"During those days Mary set out and traveled to
the hill country in haste to a town of Judah, where she
entered the house of Zechariah and greeted Elizabeth.
When Elizabeth heard Mary's greeting, the infant
leaped in her womb, and Elizabeth, filled with the Holy
Spirit, cried out in a loud voice and said, "Most blessed
are you among women, and blessed is the fruit of your
womb. And how does this happen to me, that the
mother of my Lord should come to me? For at the
moment the sound of your greeting reached my ears,
the infant in my womb leaped for joy. Blessed are you
who believed that what was spoken to you by the Lord
would be fulfilled." - Luke 1:39-45

The first child entrusted with the Cross was baby Jesus in Bethlehem, where He was rejected from the inns and born in a cold, dirty stable – laid in the manger meant as a food dish for animals. It is incredible to me to see how the Father in Heaven allowed the marks of the Cross to already leave their imprint on the life and Heart of such a little Infant, and yet in some ways only those with humble, vulnerable, open hearts like a child could ever endure the wood of the Cross at all.

"While they were there, the time came for her to have her child, and she gave birth to her firstborn son. She wrapped him in swaddling clothes and laid him in a manger, because there was no room for them in the inn. Now there were shepherds in that region living in the fields and keeping the night watch over their flock. The angel of the Lord appeared to them and the glory of the Lord shone around them, and they were struck with great fear. The angel said to them, "Do not be afraid; for behold, I proclaim to you good news of great joy that will be for all the people. For today in the city of David a savior has been born for you who is Messiah and Lord. And this will be a sign for you: you will find an infant wrapped in swaddling clothes and lying in a manger." And suddenly there was a multitude of the heavenly host with the angel,

praising God and saying: "Glory to God in the highest and on earth peace to those on whom his favor rests."

"When the angels went away from them to heaven, the shepherds said to one another, "Let us go, then, to Bethlehem to see this thing that has taken place, which the Lord has made known to us." So they went in haste and found Mary and Joseph, and the infant lying in the manger. When they saw this, they made known the message that had been told them about this child. All who heard it were amazed by what had been told them by the shepherds. And Mary kept all these things, reflecting on them in her heart. Then the shepherds returned, glorifying and praising God for all they had heard and seen, just as it had been told to them."

The suffering of Christ was predicted clearly in the words of Simeon at the Presentation in the Temple as well. Here, he spoke of Jesus as being a Child who would be contradicted and how even His Mother would have Her Heart pierced with swords right along with His Own. In the visitation of the Magi, Baby Jesus is offered gifts of gold, frankincense, and myrrh – a sign that although He was our little King, He also would be a Priest and Victim always offering the sacrifice of His Own Heart and Will to God as an oblation of Love to save all of humanity. Our Infant God was pursued by the wicked King Herod who was jealous

and fearful of Him and so wanted to slay Him right along
with all of the other Innocents – and as if such hatred itself
wasn't pain enough to His soul, the Holy Family had to flee
into Egypt by night to avoid death, and they had to embrace
all of the hardships that went along with being poor home-
less refugees in a country and among a people who were
not their own. Reflect a moment on the Christ Child in
both His majesty as well as in the sufferings He endured
from the very first moments, months, and years of His Life
on Earth:

> *"When eight days were completed for his circum-*
> *cision, he was named Jesus, the name given him by the*
> *angel before he was conceived in the womb. When the*
> *days were completed for their purification according to*
> *the law of Moses, they took him up to Jerusalem to*
> *present him to the Lord, just as it is written in the law*
> *of the Lord, "Every male that opens the womb shall be*
> *consecrated to the Lord," and to offer the sacrifice of "a*
> *pair of turtledoves or two young pigeons," in accor-*
> *dance with the dictate in the law of the Lord. Now*
> *there was a man in Jerusalem whose name was*
> *Simeon. This man was righteous and devout, awaiting*
> *the consolation of Israel, and the Holy Spirit was upon*
> *him. It had been revealed to him by the Holy Spirit*
> *that he should not see death before he had seen the*

Messiah of the Lord. He came in the Spirit into the temple; and when the parents brought in the child Jesus to perform the custom of the law in regard to him, he took him into his arms and blessed God, saying: "Now, Master, you may let your servant go in peace, according to your word, for my eyes have seen your salvation, which you prepared in sight of all the peoples, a light for revelation to the Gentiles, and glory for your people Israel." The child's father and mother were amazed at what was said about him; and Simeon blessed them and said to Mary his mother, "Behold, this child is destined for the fall and rise of many in Israel, and to be a sign that will be contradicted (and you yourself a sword will pierce) so that the thoughts of many hearts may be revealed." There was also a prophetess, Anna, the daughter of Phanuel, of the tribe of Asher. She was advanced in years, having lived seven years with her husband after her marriage, and then as a widow until she was eighty-four. She never left the temple, but worshiped night and day with fasting and prayer. And coming forward at that very time, she gave thanks to God and spoke about the child to all who were awaiting the redemption of Jerusalem."
- Luke 2:6-38

"When Jesus was born in Bethlehem of Judea, in the days of King Herod, behold, magi from the east

arrived in Jerusalem, saying, "Where is the newborn king of the Jews? We saw his star at its rising and have come to do him homage." When King Herod heard this, he was greatly troubled, and all Jerusalem with him. Assembling all the chief priests and the scribes of the people, he inquired of them where the Messiah was to be born. They said to him, "In Bethlehem of Judea, for thus it has been written through the prophet: 'And you, Bethlehem, land of Judah, are by no means least among the rulers of Judah; since from you shall come a ruler, who is to shepherd my people Israel.'" Then Herod called the magi secretly and ascertained from them the time of the star's appearance. He sent them to Bethlehem and said, "Go and search diligently for the child. When you have found him, bring me word, that I too may go and do him homage." After their audience with the king they set out. And behold, the star that they had seen at its rising preceded them, until it came and stopped over the place where the child was. They were overjoyed at seeing the star, and on entering the house they saw the child with Mary his mother. They prostrated themselves and did him homage. Then they opened their treasures and offered him gifts of gold, frankincense, and myrrh. And having been warned in a dream not to return to Herod, they departed for their country by another way.

"When they had departed, behold, the angel of the Lord appeared to Joseph in a dream and said, "Rise, take the child and his mother, flee to Egypt, and stay there until I tell you. Herod is going to search for the child to destroy him." Joseph rose and took the child and his mother by night and departed for Egypt. He stayed there until the death of Herod, that what the Lord had said through the prophet might be fulfilled, "Out of Egypt I called my son."

"When Herod realized that he had been deceived by the magi, he became furious. He ordered the massacre of all the boys in Bethlehem and its vicinity two years old and under, in accordance with the time he had ascertained from the magi. Then was fulfilled what had been said through Jeremiah the prophet: "A voice was heard in Ramah, sobbing and loud lamentation; Rachel weeping for her children, and she would not be consoled, since they were no more." - Matthew 2:1-18

The first saints to recognize and adore the Baby Jesus (besides Our Lady and St. Joseph) were Elizabeth (when she exclaims *'Blessed is the fruit of your womb!'*), the Shepherds, the Magi, and Simeon and Anna – the prophets who recognized the Christ Child in the Temple and took Him into their arms prophesizing over Him. From the very beginning, the Christ Child radiated that pure, holy Light of the Father.

"The child grew and became strong, filled with wisdom; and the favor of God."

The Child Jesus continues to astound both His parents and the elders in the Temple at age 12 both with His steadfast adherence to the will of God (and the courage of Heart He must have had to follow His Father at all costs), as well as His Wisdom in the words He spoke teaching all who listened to Him to do the same. Even still as a Child, He was embracing the Cross and holding it forth as a model and goal for all who desired authentic holiness. It must have been a real sacrifice for Him to remain behind in Jerusalem, even knowing that His parents would be worried looking for Him. And He risked much in teaching the priests – for it was not their custom to listen to preachers not educated by the Temple, let alone a Child. And yet these things made His message all the more powerful and impressive on the minds and hearts of those who listened. It is even recorded in Scripture that *'His Mother kept all of these things pondering them in Her Heart.'* (Luke 2:52) Here is how these events unfolded:

"Each year his parents went to Jerusalem for the feast of Passover, and when he was twelve years old, they went up according to festival custom. After they had completed its days, as they were returning, the boy Jesus remained behind in Jerusalem, but his parents did not know it. Thinking that he was in the caravan, they journeyed for a day and looked for him among their relatives and acquaintances, but not finding him, they returned to Jerusalem to look for him. After three days they found him in the temple, sitting in the midst of the teachers, listening to them and asking them questions, and all who heard him were astounded at his understanding and his answers. When his parents saw him, they were astonished, and his mother said to him, "Son, why have you done this to us? Your father and I have been looking for you with great anxiety." And he said to them, "Why were you looking for me? Did you not know that I must be in my Father's house?" But they did not understand what he said to them. He went down with them and came to Nazareth, and was obedient to them; and his mother kept all these things in her heart. And Jesus advanced [in] wisdom and age and favor before God and man." - Luke 2:41-52

Devotion to the Christ Child in the Writings of the Saints

Perhaps no other saint expounded with such heartfelt devotion to the Infant Jesus as St. John Chrysostom (ca. A.D. 347-407), when in the 6th and 7th homilies of his "Homilies on the Gospel of Matthew," he describes devotion to the Divine Child as he writes of the Magi honoring the newborn King:

And why did they at all worship one who was in swaddling clothes? For if He had been a grown man, one might say, that in expectation of the succor they should receive from Him, they cast themselves into a danger which they foresaw; a thing however to the utmost degree unreasonable, that the Persian, the barbarian, and one that had nothing in common with the nation of the Jews, should be willing to depart from his home, to give up country, and kindred, and friends, and that they should subject themselves to another kingdom.

But if this be foolish, what follows is much more foolish. Of what nature then is this? That after they had entered on so long a journey, and worshipped, and thrown all into confusion, they went away immediately. And what sign at all of royalty did they behold, when they saw a shed, and a manger, and a child in swaddling clothes, and a poor mother? And to whom moreover did they offer their gifts, and for what intent? Was it then usual and customary, thus to pay court to the kings that were born in every place? and did they always keep going about the whole world, worshipping them who they knew should become kings out of a low and mean estate, before they ascended the royal throne? Nay, this no one can say.

And for what purpose did they worship Him at all? If for the sake of things present, then what did they expect to receive from an infant, and a mother of mean condition?...

...Let us then also follow the magi, let us separate ourselves from our barbarian customs, and make our distance therefrom great, that we may see Christ, since they too, had they not been far from their own country, would have missed seeing Him. Let us depart from the things of earth. For so the wise men, while they were in Persia, saw but the star, but after they had departed from Persia, they beheld the Sun of Righteousness. Or rather, they would not have seen so much as the star, unless they had readily risen up from thence. Let us then also rise up; though all men be troubled, let us run to the house of the young Child; though kings, though nations, though tyrants interrupt this our path, let not our desire pass away. For so shall we thoroughly repel all the dangers that beset us. Since these too, except they had seen the young Child, would not have escaped their danger from the king. Before seeing the young Child, fears and

dangers and troubles pressed upon them from every side; but after the adoration, it is calm and security; and no longer a star but an angel receives them, having become priests from the act of adoration; for we see that they offered gifts also. Do thou therefore likewise leave the Jewish people, the troubled city, the blood-thirsty tyrant, the pomp of the world, and hasten to Bethlehem, where is the house of the spiritual Bread. For though thou be a shepherd, and come hither, thou wilt behold the young Child in an inn: though thou be a king, and approach not here, thy purple robe will profit thee nothing; though thou be one of the wise men, this will be no hindrance to thee; only let thy coming be to honor and adore, not to spurn the Son of God; only do this with trembling and joy...

Many other saints besides these mentioned above had great devotion to the Child Jesus. Most famously St. Therese of Lisieux (of the Child Jesus) took her name from Him. But The Divine Infant appeared to many saints and drew the love of their heart over the centuries. The Baby Jesus appeared in the arms of His Mother one day to St. Rose of Lima and offered her the mystical espousals, saying: ***"Rose of My heart, be My spouse!"*** St. Teresa of Avila always traveled with her statue of the Infant Jesus when she was establishing new convents. One day Teresa of Avila was coming down the steps of her convent when she

saw a beautiful young boy. The Child spoke to her and
said: *"Who are you?"* So Teresa answered: *"I am Teresa of
Jesus and who are you?"* The Child answered with a play of
words: *"I am Jesus of Teresa!"* and then He disappeared. And the Infant appeared to several of them
allowing them to hold Him in their arms – including St.
Anthony of Padua, St. Christopher, St. Francis of Assisi, St
Stanislaus Kostka, St. Catherine of Bologna, St. Gemma, St.
Faustina and St. Padre Pio.

The Infant of Prague

Perhaps the most famous devotion to the Infant Jesus
has taken the form in His Title 'The Infant of Prague'. This
is from Prague, Czech Republic, where a statue (Spanish in
origin) ended up in its present country when it was taken
there as a wedding gift given to a Spanish woman upon her
marriage to a Czech nobleman. It passed down through
that family and was eventually given to the Discalced
Carmelites there.

In 1628, the Carmelites had to escape the area when the
Saxons, and then the Swedes, attacked. A priest named
Father Cyril returned to Prague in 1638 and found the
statue lying in what was left of the church, its arms broken.
He placed it back in the oratory for veneration and, while
praying near it one day, heard the voice of the Infant Jesus
say to Him, **"Have pity on Me and I will have pity on you.**

Give Me My hands and I will give you peace. The more you honor Me, the more I will bless you". In that war-torn era, the priest didn't have the money to carry out that wish, so prayed for guidance. He heard the Child Jesus again, **"Place Me near the entrance of the sacristy and you will receive aid."** And so, it happened. Within a few days, a rich man came by and offered to repair the statue.

The statue became known for its association with the miraculous, including healings and, especially, for the protection of the church through so many wars that followed. Many benefits are said to come to those who worship Christ under His title of the "Infant of Prague," and there are prayers and novenas to Him under this name.

El Santo Niño de Atocha

In Mexico, the Holy Child is known under various titles, the most famous of which is El Santo Niño de Atocha. In the Mexican State of Zacatecas are two towns with two shrines: the more famous Fresnillo, home of the "Blue Santo Niño," and Plateros, where the "Pink Santo Niño" is found. The statues of the Infant are dressed in the attire of a pilgrim: brimmed hat, cape, and a scallop shell - the pilgrim's badge indicating pilgrimage to Compostela in Spain where the relics of St. James the Greater can be found. The Child Jesus carries a basket of food, and a pilgrim's staff to which are fasted a gourd (to hold water) and wheat.

The devotion originated in Atocha, Spain when the Moors invaded and took many Christians as prisoners. The Christians were not allowed visitors and began to fear for their very lives as they lacked food and anyone to bring them some. After praying intensely for relief, the Christ Child appeared dressed in the attire described above and bearing a basket of food and a container of water, neither of which were depleted until they were no longer needed.

El Santo Niño de Atocha is most often invoked for healing, especially of children. Pilgrims to his shrines leave children's shoes, a custom born in the folk tale that the Child wears out His own as He goes about at night secretly visiting sick children in order to heal them.

In Conclusion

As we see the great depth in the mystery of God's Love in the Christ Child, as well as the devotion of the saints over the years (and the Baby Jesus' Divine intervention in their lives), it is made obvious to all that no greater example of holiness could be held up for children than that of Little Jesus Himself. Resplendent in virtue He desires to pour out upon all souls (both old and young) the newness and freshness of life lived in constant union with the heavenly Father. The Baby Jesus calls to each one of us to learn to be like Him, for it was precisely His simplicity, innocence, humility, purity, strength, trust, faith, and love that He was pleading for us to imitate when He said as an adult, *"Learn from Me, for I am meek and humble of Heart..."* (Mt. 11:29)

■■

Prayer to the Infant of Prague

Divine Infant Jesus, I adore Thy Cross, and I accept all the crosses Thou wilt be pleased to send me. Adorable Trinity, I offer Thee, for the glory of the Holy Name of God, all the adorations of the Sacred Heart of the Holy Infant Jesus.

The Word was made flesh,
And dwelt among us.

Holy Infant Jesus of Prague,
Bless and protect us. Amen.

Chapter 3

The Infant Mary (Maria Bambina)

Besides Jesus, there has never been a more perfect Child
than the Infant Mary. She was immaculately conceived,
which means that Her Heart was so unstained by sin (both
original and actual sin) that from the first moments of Her
existence, Her Heart was a garden castle where the Holy
Trinity could dwell in full.

We adore Jesus in His Divine Childhood. In the same
way, we venerate Mary in her childhood. Mary is the
Woman chosen by God at the beginning of time in Genesis
(Genesis 3:15) to bring forth the Savior – and to do that She
was immaculately conceived. This means that God took the
merits of Christ's Passion and went back in time and
applied them to Our Lady when She was conceived. The
redemption of Jesus was applied earlier in time because He
is eternal and outside of time. By doing this, God was
creating a perfect Tabernacle (the first home – being that of
Our Mother's womb) for His Divine Son. This means that
Our Lady was Immaculate – perfect – and that Her Infant
Heart never changed throughout Her life (like ours becomes stained through sin and needs Confession and the
Sacraments to renew it). Mary's Immaculate Heart is the
same at Her birth as it was under Calvary. Mary's Heart
pierced with swords under the cross was an Infant Heart –
total in Her innocence and purity pierced with pain. Purity
is the presence of God – and Our Lady called *'full of grace'*
by the angel Gabriel when He visited Her at the Annun-

ciation was most pure and most humble, therefore making Her so full of the presence of God.

This perfect Heart of the Child Mary is foreshadowed by the Book of Wisdom 7: 22-30:

"For in her is a spirit intelligent, holy, unique, manifold, subtle, agile, clear, unstained, certain, never harmful, loving the good, keen, unhampered, beneficent, kindly, firm, secure, tranquil, all-powerful, all-seeing, and pervading all spirits, though they be intelligent, pure and very subtle. For Wisdom is mobile beyond all motion, and she penetrates and pervades all things by reason of her purity. For she is a breath of the might of God and a pure emanation of the glory of the Almighty; therefore nothing defiled can enter into her. For she is the reflection of eternal light, the spotless mirror of the power of God, the image of his goodness. Although she is one, she can do all things, and she renews everything while herself purduring; Passing into holy souls from age to age, she produces friends of God and prophets. For God loves nothing so much as the one who dwells with Wisdom. For she is fairer than the sun and surpasses every constellation of the stars. Compared to light, she is found more radiant; though night supplants light, wickedness does not prevail over Wisdom."

For centuries, the Church has celebrated Mary's Nativity on 8 September – Hers being one of only three birthdays so honored, the other two being those of Jesus and His Precursor (St. John the Baptist). All three of these were born without the stain of original sin. St. John was filled with the Holy Spirit while in his mother's womb (Luke 1:13-17, 44) whereas Jesus and Mary were *conceived* full of grace.

The Feast of the Birth of Mary was first celebrated in the East by the Church of Jerusalem. In the fifth century, a Byzantine church was erected there, on the spot where a tradition says the house of Sts. Anne and Joachim once stood and became a focal point for her birthday celebration. Unfortunately, the original church was decimated during the Crusades. A new church was later built on that spot; this one still stands today and is a center of pilgrimage. The Catholic Church adopted this joyful feast by the seventh century by Pope Sergius I and the feast was celebrated every September 8.

On the other hand, the Feast of the Most Holy Name of Mary commemorates the day the Blessed Virgin was named a few days after her birth in accordance with the Jewish Law. The Feast was originated in Spain and was approved by the Holy See in 1513 then later extended to the whole Church by Pope Innocent XI in 1683 in thanksgiving to Our Lady for the Victory of John III Sobieski, King of Poland, over the Turks, who were besieging Vienna and threatening the West. This Feast of the Holy Name of Mary is celebrated each year on September 12th.

The Feast of the Presentation of Mary that is celebrated every November 21st is also very ancient, going back to the sixth century in the Eastern Orthodox Church and it is one of the thirteen Great Feasts of the Church, often depicted in icons. The Catholic Church, however, did not adopt it until the fourteenth century.

Most of what we know of Our Lady's childhood is known through apocryphal sources and the writings of mystic saints like St. Bridget of Sweden, Blessed Anne Katherina Emmerich and Venerable Maria de Agreda, who were favored with the visions of Her childhood. From these works, we were able to have a glimpse of the early life of the Blessed Virgin Mary. We learn that her parents were St. Anne and St. Joachim (whose Feasts we celebrate on July 26th), that She was born late in their life and dedicated to the Temple at an early age. Here we can read in St. Bridget's own words what Our Lady revealed to Her about Her Childhood:

The Childhood, Life and Miracles of the Virgin Mary in her own words revealed to St. Bridget

"*I am the Queen of Heaven. Love my Son, for he is most worthy; when you have him, you have all that is worthwhile. He is also most desirable; when you have him, you have all that is desirable. Love him, too, for he is most virtuous; when you have him, you have every virtue. I want to tell you how wonderful his love for my body and soul was and how much he honored my name. My Son loved me before I loved him, since he is my Creator.*

He united my father and mother in a marriage so chaste that there could not be found a more chaste marriage at that time. They never wanted to come together except in accordance with the Law, and only then with the intention to bring forth offspring.

When an angel revealed to them that they would give birth to the Virgin from whom the salvation of the world would come, they would rather have died than to come together in carnal love; lust was dead in them. I assure you that when they did come together, it was because of divine love and because of the angel's message, not out of carnal desire, but against their will and out of a holy love for God. In this way, my flesh was put together by their seed and through divine love. Then, when my body had been made and formed, God infused the created soul into it from his divinity, and the soul was immediately sanctified along with the body, and the angels guarded and served it day and night. When my soul was sanctified and joined to its body, my mother felt such great joy that it would have been impossible to describe it!

Afterwards, when my lifetime had been accomplished, my Son first raised up my soul - for it was the mistress of the body - to a more excellent place than others in heaven, right next to his Divinity. Later, he also raised up my body in such a manner that no other creature's body is so close to God as mine. See how much my Son loved my soul and body! Yet, there are some people with a malevolent spirit who deny that I was assumed into Heaven, body and soul, and also others who simply do not know any better. But this is a most certain truth: I, with body and soul, was assumed to the Divinity!

Hear now how much my Son honored my name! My name is Mary, as it is said in the Gospel. When the angels hear this name, they rejoice in their mind and thank God for the great mercy that he worked through me and with me and because they see my Son's Humanity glorified in his Divinity. Those within the fire of purgatory rejoice exceedingly, just like a sick and bedridden man does if he receives a word of comfort that pleases his soul: he is suddenly overjoyed! When the good angels hear my name, they immediately move closer to the righteous for whom they are guardians, and rejoice over their progress in good deeds and virtues.

All humans have been given both good angels for their protection, and bad angels to test them. The good angels are not separated from God; they serve the soul without leaving God. They are constantly in his sight. Yet they work to inflame and incite the soul to do good. All the demons, however, shudder with fear at the name of Mary! When they hear the name, "Mary", they immediately release a soul out of the claws with which they had held her. Just as a bird or hawk, with its claws and beak embedded into its prey, releases it immediately if it hears a sound, but soon returns when it sees that no action follows, so do the demons - frightened when they hear my name – release the soul. But they return and fly back as fast as an arrow if no improvement follows.

No one is so cold in his love of God (unless he is damned) that he will not experience the devil releasing him from his habitual sins if only he invokes my name with the true intention of never returning to his evil deeds. The devil will never return to him unless he resumes the will to commit mortal sins. Sometimes, though, the devil is allowed to trouble him for the sake of his greater reward. However, the devil shall never own him.

"I am the Queen of Heaven, the Mother of God. I told you to wear a brooch on your chest. I will now show you more fully how, from the beginning, when I first

heard and understood that God existed, I always, and with fear, was concerned about my salvation and my observance of his commandments. But when I learned more about God - that he was my Creator and the judge of all my actions - I loved him more dearly, and I was constantly fearful and watchful so as to not offend him by word or deed.

Later, when I heard that he had given the Law and the commandments to the people and worked such great miracles through them, I made a firm decision in my soul to never love anything but him, and all worldly things became most bitter to me. When still later I heard that God himself would redeem the world and be born of a Virgin, I was seized by such great love for him that I thought of nothing but God and desired nothing but him. I withdrew myself, as much as I was able, from the conversation and presence of parents and friends, and I gave away all my possessions to the poor, and kept nothing for myself but meager food and clothing.

Nothing was pleasing to me but God! I always wished in my heart to live until the time of his birth, and perhaps, deserve to become the unworthy handmaid of the Mother of God. I also promised in my heart to keep my virginity, if this was acceptable to him, and to have no possessions in the world. However, if God wanted otherwise, my will was that his will, not mine, be done; for I believed that he could do all things and wanted nothing but what was beneficial and best for me. Therefore, I entrusted all my will to him.

When the time approached for the virgins to be presented in the temple of the Lord, I was also among them due to the devout compliance of my parents to the Law. I thought to myself that nothing was impossible for God, and since he knew that I wanted and desired nothing but him, I knew that he could protect my virginity, if it pleased him. However, if not, I wanted his will to be done. After I had heard all the commandments in the temple, I returned home, burning even more now than ever before with the love of God, being inflamed daily with new fires and desires of love.

For this reason, I withdrew myself even more from everyone, and was alone day and night, fearing greatly, and most of all, that my mouth should say anything, or my ears hear anything against the will of my God, or that my eyes see anything alluring or harmful. I was also afraid in the silence, and very worried that I might be silent about things of which I should, instead, have spoken.

While I was worried in my heart like this, alone by myself and placing all my hope in God, an inspiration about God's great power came over me, and I recalled how the angels and everything created serve him, and how his glory is indescribable and unlimited. While I was thus fascinated by this thought, I saw three wonderful things: I saw a star, but not the kind that shines in the sky; I saw a light, but not the kind that shines in this world; I smelled a fragrance, but not of herbs or anything else of this world. It was most delightful and truly indescribable, and it filled me up so completely that I jubilated with joy!

After this, I immediately heard a voice - but not from a human mouth - and when I heard it, I shuddered with the great fear that it might be an illusion, or a mockery by an evil spirit. But shortly after this, an angel of God appeared before me; he was like the most handsome of men, but not in the flesh as is the body of a created man, and he said to me: 'Hail, full of grace, the Lord is with thee!' When I heard this, I wondered what he meant and why he had come to me with such a greeting, for I knew and believed that I was unworthy of any such thing - or any good thing! However, I also knew that nothing is impossible for God, if he desires it.

Then the angel spoke again: 'The child to be born in you is holy and will be called the Son of God. May his will be done as it pleases him.' But, not even then did I consider myself worthy, and I did not ask the angel why, or when, this would happen. Instead I asked him how it could be that I, an unworthy maiden, who did not know any man, should become the Mother of God. The angel answered me (as I have just said): 'Nothing is impossible for God, for whatever he wants to do will be done.'

When I had heard these words of the angel, I felt the most fervent desire to become the Mother of God, and my soul spoke out of love and desire, saying: 'See, here I am; your will be done in me!' With these words, my Son was conceived in my womb to the indescribable joy of my soul and my every limb! While I had him in my womb, I bore him without any pain, without any heaviness or discomfort. I humbled myself in all things, knowing that he whom I bore was the Almighty!..."

The Maria Bambina in Milan, Italy

Devotion to the Infant Mary has also spread through pious devotion of the priests (Popes), religious, and laity of the Church. As far back as 1007, the people of Milan, Italy, built a church dedicated to the Maria Bambina. The church "Santa Maria Fulcorina" was dedicated to the "Mystery of the Nativity of Mary" and eventually became the cathedral church of Milan. The present-day cathedral was built and was later consecrated by St. Charles Borromeo in A.D. 1572 and dedicated to "Mariae Nascenti" - "The Nativity of

Mary." This city, then, became one of the centers of devotion to the Child Mary. In 1251, the Pope granted special indulgences to anyone who visited that church on September 8, the feast of Her birthday.

The devotion to the Infant Mary spread even further in Italy when in 1735 a religious sister made a wax image of Our Lady as a baby – this statue traveled around to several locations and in 1884 ended up in a convent of sisters. The statue had faded to grey, but while in the custody of these sisters a huge miracle of healing of a couple of the infirm sisters happened through the Infant Mary's intercession – and when this happened, lively color returned to the faded image. There is now a great church dedicated to the Infant Mary in that place. In November 1984, Pope John Paul II made a pilgrimage to this convent Church saying to the Sisters of Charity of Milan at their Motherhouse, *"This mystery [of the Holy Childhood of Mary] seems to be very little known. I think you have a great task........ to deepen the appreciation of the mystery of Mary's childhood."*

An Apparition in Mexico

Devotion to the Infant Mary sprang up as well in 1840 in Mexico City to a sister who knew nothing about these churches and statues in Milan. On January 6, 1840, the Feast of the Epiphany of Our Lord, Sister Magdalena de San José, a Franciscan Conceptionist sister, knelt before a nativity scene in her convent in Mexico City, contemplating the Christ Child in the manger. An inspiration came to her during her prayers that there would be a similar devotion that will be accorded to the Child Mary. Suddenly, a lovely little girl appeared before her, dressed like a tiny princess and reclining in thin air. Sister Magdalena immediately knew that this beautiful child was the Virgin Mary, appearing to her in the form of a baby. The Infant Mary spoke to her giving her promise to those who will have a devotion to her Childhood: *"I will grant great graces to whoever honors me in my infancy"*.

The astonished nun went to the abbess and told her of her vision and her desire to promote devotion to little Mary. The abbess did not quite share Sister Magdalena's excitement, so the devotion was not promoted right away.

But Sister Magdalena kept praying for God to bring it about. Eventually, Sister Magdalena did receive permission to ask a local sculptor to fashion a statue of the Infant Mary. Once she received the image, she began to spread the devotion. Many people experienced miracles through the intercession of little Mary, but others questioned the suitability of such a devotion. Yet after years of careful study, Pope Gregory XVI approved the devotion and even granted indulgences to those who practiced it in 1846.

Devotion to the Child Mary in Malta

Another famed Shrine dedicated to the Child Mary was located in Senglea, Malta, where the Child Mary became the focal point of the Maltese devotions. The origin of the statue dated back in 1618 where, according to pious tradition, a statue of Our Lady was found floating together with other wreckage from a galleon (sailing ship), A captain of an Austrian galley, on reaching the vicinity of those islands, caught sight of the statue floating among the wreckage and fished it out of the sea, donating it to the nearest island which was Senglea in Malta. The devotion to the Child Mary in Senglea was strong in the area, most especially during the month of September.

The devotion to the Infant Mary is also very popular in the Philippines, having been brought there by Spanish Missionaries.

The Devotion of the Saints

Besides the revelations concerning Our Lady's infancy to several mystics and saints in the Church, there have been several other saints particularly devoted to Our Lady in Her Infancy. St. John Eudes wrote a beautiful Litany to the Infant Mary. St. Padre Pio and St. Joseph of Cupertino had a statue of the Maria Bambina in their private oratories. St. Hannibal Mary Di Francia of the Rogationist Order loved the child Mary with an ardent love and saw to it that in all his houses She was venerated with special devotion. At the hour of his death, the Blessed Lady wanted to give him a sign of Her heavenly approval to the devotion. One morning, a few days before his death, his face suddenly lit up, and he stared out a point in the room, exclaiming as though rapt: *"Brother, look!... Look how beautiful She is! Look at the beautiful Child Mary!..."* And he remained engrossed in the sweet vision.

Another foundress saint was known for her devotion to the Child Mary, notably Saint Jeanne de Lestonnac of the Order of the Company of Mary. Saint Jeanne was known for her active propagation to the devotion to the Child Mary by placing images of the Niña in the schools that were administered by her religious congregation. These schools held devotional activities like processions and other Marian devotions every November 21, the Feast of the Presentation of Mary since 1610 when she initiated this tradition in the first school opened in Bordeaux, France. To express gratitude to God for all that had been accomplished in spite of difficulties and for the students to offer their lives to the Lord through the intercession of Mary, it was Saint Jeanne's wish that this feast be celebrated in all Company of Mary schools for all time and that it become a permanent tradition. This tradition was carried over to Vigo, Spain, and in Japan where the Company of Mary also established their schools in those countries.

The Infant Mary as a Model for All

Devotion to the Maria Bambina (the Infant Mary) remains with us today as a model and inspiration for all – both children and adults alike. This sweet, little Immaculate One is a mighty intercessor against all evil. Her Heart is a Star to light our way to heaven. Her Heart is the voice of purity interceding for us before God. Her tiny Heart is a fortress against evil because of its purity. Her dedication to God is full through and through. Mary's 'Fiat' to the Angel in the Annunciation is not something new to Her – for She prayed 'Fiat' all of the days of Her life, even up unto (and through) the Cross with Her Son Jesus. In the midst of the greatest evil of the Passion and Death of Jesus, Her innocence and faith intercede for us before God. Her Love is stalwartly and resilient through all pain and death.

Our Lady was conceived in perfect purity and preserved that perfect purity by never choosing sin. In this, She is a great example for all children as they progress through life to remain faithful in their commitment to God, no matter how they grow and mature into adults. She is an example for adults, inspiring us to return to littleness, humility, and pure love in all we say and do – in how we pray – in how we interact with heaven and those we encounter on earth.

■■■

Novena Prayer to the Maria Bambina (Infant Mary)

Holy Child Mary of the royal house of David, Queen of the angels, Mother of grace and love, I greet you with all my heart. Obtain for me the grace to love the Lord faithfully during all the days of my life. Obtain for me, too, a great devotion to you, who are the first creature of God's love.

Hail Mary, full of grace................

O heavenly Child Mary, who like a pure dove was born immaculate and beautiful, true prodigy of the wisdom of God, my soul rejoices in you. Oh! Do help me to preserve the angelic virtue of purity at the cost of any sacrifice.

Hail Mary, full of grace................

Hail, lovely and holy Child, spiritual garden of delight,

where, on the day of the Incarnation, the tree of life was planted, assist me to avoid the poisonous fruit of vanity and pleasures of the world. Help me to engraft into my soul the thoughts, feelings, and virtues of your divine Son.

Hail Mary, full of grace..............

Hail, admirable Child Mary, Mystical Rose, closed garden, open only to the heavenly Spouse. O Lily of paradise, make me love the humble and hidden life; let the heavenly Spouse find the gate of my heart always open to the loving calls of His graces and inspiration.

Hail Mary, full of grace..............

Holy Child Mary, mystical dawn, gate of heaven, you are my trust and hope. O powerful advocate, from your cradle stretch out your hand, support me on the path of life. Make me serve God with ardor and constancy until death and so reach an eternity with you.

Hail Mary, full of grace..............

Prayer:

Blessed Child Mary, destined to be the Mother of God and our loving Mother, by the heavenly graces you lavish upon us, mercifully listen to my supplications. In the needs which press upon me from every side and especially in my present tribulation, I place all my trust in you.

O holy Child, by the privileges granted to you alone and by the merits which you have acquired, show that the source of spiritual favors and the continuous benefits which you dispense are inexhaustible, because your power with the Heart of God is unlimited.

Deign through the immense profusion of graces with which the Most High has enriched you from the first moment of your Immaculate Conception, grant me, O Celestial Child, my petition, and I shall eternally praise the goodness of your Immaculate Heart.

I M P R I M A T U R

In Curia Archiep. Mediolani

31 August 1931

Can. CAVEZZALI, Pro Vic. Gen

Chapter 4

Children in Scripture

"In the beginning was the Word, and the Word was with God, and the Word was God. He was in the beginning with God. All things came to be through him, and without him nothing came to be. What came to be through him was life, and this life was the light of the human race; the light shines in the darkness, and the darkness has not overcome it." (John 1:1-5)

All was created through the Word.

At the beginning of time, the Father spoke the Word, *'Let there be Light,'* (Gen 1:3) and there was light. Many years later when he was creating you and me, He said similar words. He said, *"Let there be Mary."* And there was "Mary". He said, *"Let there be Samuel," "Let there be Matthew," "Let there be John," "Let there be Emma," "Let there be Elizabeth,"* and suddenly there was "Samuel," "Matthew," "John," "Emma" and "Elizabeth". This Scripture from the beginning of St. John's Gospel said that all things came to be through Him – which means each and every soul, every child created in his mother's womb, came to be through the Word of God – came to be through Jesus, Who was the *"Word made Flesh."*

"He was in the world and the world came to be through him, but the world did not know him. He came to what

was his own, but his own people did not accept him. But to those who did accept him he gave power to become children of God, to those who believe in his name, who were born not by natural generation nor by human choice nor by a man's decision but of God. And the Word became flesh and made his dwelling among us, and we saw his glory, the glory as of the Father's only Son, full of grace and truth." (John 1:10-14)

What is most striking here is to see how each person finds their original identity in Jesus Christ the Word. It is through the Word of God – made flesh in Jesus, received in the Eucharist, and spoken in Scripture – that each of us are created and recreated to be the children of God who will reign with Him for eternity. Because of this, one can see clearly the high dignity of each human being – even as a child – and the great respect and holiness of each human life even from conception – and especially found in one's childhood when they are most pure and holy, freshly baptized and still unable to sin (or choose anything that breaks his tiny heart from the Heart of the Father).

The beauty of Scripture in the lives of children finds its source first and foremost in the creation of a child's body and soul through the Word of God (the same Word of God Who became Flesh and dwelt among us). So, often (too often, I fear), people do not recognize the creative power of the Second Person of the Trinity as being the instrument through which one was created (like St. John's Gospel alludes to), but nonetheless, each child is created in the image and likeness of God through the Word of God.

> *"Then God said: Let us make human beings in our image, after our likeness. Let them have dominion over the fish of the sea, the birds of the air, the tame animals, all the wild animals, and all the creatures that crawl on the earth. God created mankind in his image; in the image of God he created them; male and female he created them"* (Genesis 1:26-27)

In this, we see how each child finds his or her original dignity, as well as his or her restored dignity (after a person falls in sin) in the Word of God, Who is Jesus Christ.

We also see in this passage from Genesis how the imprint of the Incarnate Word is pressed upon the heart and soul of each human creature made by God. We are made *"in His image and likeness."* And what's more than just that, we are not created simply as replicas of Him, but uniquely and diverse as the attributes of God. From the beginning of our existence God has fashioned us (knowing every tiny detail about our hair and eyes, our talents, and our gifts) for a purpose. We are created purposefully by God, through Christ, for a specific vocation. And by reflecting on all of these things together, we see that the spiritual formation of children is simply uncovering (like a sculptor chiseling away at marble to uncover a statue) what God already placed within a child from the beginning. To understand these mysteries more deeply, we look at Psalm 139 where the Psalmist describes how each soul is created in Love, by Love and for Love:

"LORD, you have probed me, you know me: you know when I sit and stand;
You understand my thoughts from afar.
You sift through my travels and my rest; with all my ways you are familiar.
Even before a word is on my tongue, LORD, you know it all.

Behind and before you encircle me and rest your hand upon me.
Such knowledge is too wonderful for me, far too lofty for me to reach.
Where can I go from your spirit? From your presence, where can I flee?
If I ascend to the heavens, you are there; if I lie down in Sheol, there you are.
If I take the wings of dawn and dwell beyond the sea,

*Even there your hand guides me, your right hand holds
me fast.*

*If I say, "Surely darkness shall hide me, and night shall
be my light"—*

*Darkness is not dark for you, and night shines as the
day.*

Darkness and light are but one.

*You formed my inmost being; you knit me in my
mother's womb.*

*I praise you, because I am wonderfully made;
wonderful are your works!*

*My very self you know. My bones are not hidden from
you, When I was being made in secret, fashioned in
the depths of the earth.*

*Your eyes saw me unformed; in your book all are
written down;*

my days were shaped, before one came to be." (Psalm
139: 1-16)

Another Scripture that speaks powerfully to the creation of
each human soul as a masterpiece of God's Love and pre-
destined for salvation through the Blood and Passion of
Jesus poured out for him or her on the Cross (as long as
their free will accepts that gift of salvation) is found in
Isaiah. This Scripture, when read slowly and meditated on

in prayer, infuses healing grace into the one reading or listening to it as it reiterates the fact that we were created on purpose by God in love. We are, moreover, protected by His love, saved by His love, fortified by His love, and destined to an eternity dwelling with His love. It is almost impossible to encounter these impressive words of Scripture and not be transformed by the efficacious grace God etches upon the heart as they are embraced by them:

"But now, thus says the LORD, who created you, Jacob, and formed you, Israel: Do not fear, for I have redeemed you; I have called you by name: you are mine. When you pass through waters, I will be with you; through rivers, you shall not be swept away. When you walk through fire, you shall not be burned, nor will flames consume you. For I, the LORD, am your God, the Holy One of Israel, your savior. I give Egypt as ransom for you, Ethiopia and Seba in exchange for you. Because you are precious in my eyes and honored, and I love you, I give people in return for you and nations in exchange for your life.

Fear not, for I am with you; from the east I will bring back your offspring, from the west I will gather you. I will say to the north: Give them up! and to the south: Do not hold them! Bring back my sons from afar, and my daughters from the ends of the earth: All who are called by my name I created for my glory; I formed them, made them." (Isaiah 43:1-7)

Scripture is not only the source of every human heart's creation and the means by which the Lord uses to recreate us (after the fall of sin) in Christ, but it is also the Light – the example – held up as a model for us to face, conform to, and follow as the road that leads to heaven. One of my favorite Scripture passages that inspires the littleness of humility, docility, surrender, and trust needed in a human heart to find its way to heaven is presented in Psalm 131:

> "*LORD, my heart is not proud; nor are my eyes haughty.*
> *I do not busy myself with great matters, with things too sublime for me*
> *Rather, I have stilled my soul, Like a weaned child to its mother,*
> *weaned is my soul. Israel, hope in the LORD, now and forever.*" (Psalm 131)

In this Scripture, the Lord is inspiring in the heart of the Psalmist (and upon each one of us who reads and prays these words) the model of a newborn baby as the ideal stance of a soul seeking union with God in the spiritual life. This path set forth by God in this Scripture uses a small child as the paradigm for a soul to follow if it wants to reach heaven. And this example given to us is the opposite of all that the world puts forth as desirable. In Psalm 131, we are inspired to be little, as opposed to big and 'important'. We are inspired to be empty of self, as opposed to proud, haughty, selfish, and vain. We are inspired to rest in God, as opposed to work oneself to death for visible success, efficiency, gain. We are inspired to be content with the core of the purpose of our being created by God, which is to *be still and simply know Him*' (Psalm 46:10) and to love Him and be beloved by Him, as we serve Him through little breaths and acts of grace responding to His Love. It draws one's focus back to what is most important – living simple faith, love, and hope – in the midst of a world that has forgotten what it means to be a child of God.

These Scriptures are important not only in teaching a child about his or her own dignity and in forming him or her to live and grow as a child of God, but also in reforming us adults to be like children, emptied of self-importance and satisfied with being children of God. Lest we miss these things while reading these Scriptures of the Old Testament, God loudly exclaims these same truths clearly in the New Testament in the clear words and example of Jesus Christ Himself. In the Gospel of Matthew, we encounter several lessons where the Lord Jesus used children as the blueprint the disciples should follow if they want to enter the Kingdom of Heaven. First, we see in Matthew 18:

"At that time the disciples approached Jesus and said, "Who is the greatest in the kingdom of heaven?" <u>He called a child over, placed it in their midst, and said, "Amen, I say to you, unless you turn and become like children, you will not enter the kingdom of heaven. Whoever humbles himself like this child is the greatest in the kingdom of heaven. And whoever receives one child such as this in my name receives me.</u> Whoever causes one of these little ones who believe in me to sin, it would be better for him to have a great millstone hung around his neck and to be drowned in the depths of the sea." (Matthew 18:1-6)

These are powerful words of Christ in praise of children. He teaches adult men that they must become like children to enter heaven. They must use the model of a child's humility to get into heaven. If the Lord Jesus is telling His apostles and disciples to imitate a child, how much more should we use these words in our formation of children. Instead of teaching children to become proud, competitive, self-reliant, selfish, etc., we should encourage them to preserve and grow in their natural childlike gifts and tendencies, even as they mature in age. We see here the importance of encouraging them to remain little and humble, docile, surrendered, and trustworthy, simple and pure before the light of God all of the days of their lives.

The disciples obviously did not grasp what Jesus was trying to teach to them because in the following chapter of the Gospel of Matthew Jesus has to repeat the lesson. In this story, children are trying to get to Jesus, and the apostles are preventing them. Once again, Jesus tries to change their way of thinking, and He holds up what the disciples disdain as annoying or superfluous (the presence of children at their meeting) as important models for their behavior. Here Jesus says:

> *"Let the little children come to me, and do not hinder them, for the kingdom of heaven belongs to such as these."* (Matthew 19:14)

We must keep these Scriptures as lanterns to guide our way as we embark on the great work of forming the little hearts and souls of the children of this world for Christ. We are to teach them not to be greater, bigger, or better – but instead simply to preserve the goodness they innately are in their littleness – teaching them in some ways to grow without changing, to go forward to lead and guide without conforming to the world, to adhere closer and closer to Christ with every step they take and breath they breathe on earth. In this way, they will best glorify God. For Scripture says:

"O LORD, our Lord, how awesome is your name through all the earth! I will sing of your majesty above the heavens with the mouths of babes and infants. You have established a bulwark against your foes, to silence enemy and avenger." (Psalm 8:2-3)

And

"Out of the mouths of babes you have found perfect praise..." (Matthew 21:16)

Chapter 5

Saints Who Were Children and Who Were Dedicated to the Passion of Christ

The young shepherdess who saw Our Lady in Lourdes, St. Bernadette, found solace in her suffering by turning her eyes to Our Lord.

"O Jesus, Jesus," she prayed, "I no longer feel my cross when I think of yours. Let the crucifix be not only in my eyes and on my breast, but in my heart. Let my crucified heart sink forever into Thine..."

As we meditate on the lives and virtues of the two holiest children who ever lived (Jesus and Mary), we may begin to excuse others from trying to imitate them – saying that no child without the perfection of grace as these two creatures had would be able to attain such holiness. And although Jesus in His Divinity is way beyond us in sanctity, He was also fully human which means he encountered the same sufferings and temptations that every child does, and He conquered these things through adhering to His Father's Will and always following Love.

Our Lady also was immaculately conceived, meaning that she was totally free from the stain and weakness of sin – and yet, being only human, She, too, was subject to temptations to vice and through the merit of Her Own strength of will cooperating with grace was able to conquer all evil.

And yet I want to offer here to the reader the additional examples of the saints who went before us – particularly saints who *were children* – children who embraced the Cross like (and with) Jesus and Mary and left behind their short, little lives a legacy of love that shines a brilliant light for us to follow to heaven. Sometimes adults form children to be holy – but some saintly children form adults through their example. Who were some of these child saints who so bravely lived heroic virtue and quickly won the heavenly crown barely after their feet began to walk on earth? I present these following examples to inspire you in forming the children in your lives to love and serve Jesus as fully as they did.

St. Bernadette from Lourdes (January 7, 1844 - April 16, 1879) was not only blessed with heavenly apparitions of Our Lady as a child but followed the directives and example of Our Lady's love so fully that she quickly reached the heights of perfection and was taken to heaven. St. Bernadette was known as a truthful, devoted child. She obviously was obedient, for when the Blessed Mother told her to dig in the dry ground to find a stream of healing water, she immediately obeyed (even against all reason). She suffered greatly at the hands of the authorities (and her family) who did not believe what they thought to be childish tales – and her only response was to intensify her prayers and sacrifices to the Lady who appeared asking for

'Penance Penance Penance' declaring that She was 'the Immaculate Conception.' Here are some quotes from St. Bernadette on suffering:

"O Jesus, I would rather die a thousand deaths than be unfaithful to you!"

"I must die to myself continually and accept trials without complaining. I work, I suffer and I love with no other witness than his heart. Anyone who is not prepared to suffer all for the Beloved and to do his will in all things is not worthy of the sweet name of Friend, for here below, Love without suffering does not exist."

"I shall spend every moment loving. One who loves does not notice her trials; or perhaps more accurately, she is able to love them. I shall do everything for Heaven, my true home. There I shall find my Mother in all the splendor of her glory. I shall delight with her in the joy of Jesus himself in perfect safety."

"Oh my Mother, to you I sacrifice all other attachments so that my heart may belong entirely to you and to my Jesus."

"O My God, I beg You, by Your loneliness, not that You may spare me affliction, but that You may not abandon me in it. When I encounter affliction, teach me to see You in it as my sole comforter. Let affliction strengthen my faith, fortify my hope, and purify my love. Grant me the grace to see Your hand in my affliction, and to desire no other comforter but You."

"What will be the crown of those who, humble within and humiliated without, have imitated the humility of our Savior in all its fullness!"

"I must be holy, because my Jesus wants it."

Sts. Jacinta, Francisco, and Lucia from Fatima are similar examples of holiness in childhood. Our Lady appeared to them (also shepherds like St. Bernadette) asking for prayers and penance for the conversion of souls (specifically Russia) and for the ultimate Triumph of Her Immaculate Heart in the World. The children were struck deeply to the heart by what Our Lady spoke to them and showed them in visions – of heaven, hell, and purgatory. Willing to embrace great sacrifice for the salvation of the souls they saw doomed to eternal perdition, the three all lived heroically holy lives of faith, obedience, prayer, sacrifice, and love. No persecution or threats by the authorities could deter them from the path laid before them by the Mother of God. St. Jacinta and St. Francesco died shortly after the visions ended, while St. Lucia remained long on earth to extend her prayers, sacrifices, and aid in helping spread the message of Fatima (even while being hidden away in a convent).

St. Jacinta Marto (March 11, 1910 - February 20, 1920)
St. Francisco Marto (June 11, 1908 - April 4, 1919)
St. Lúcia de Jesus Rosa dos Santos, O.C.D. (March 28,
1907 – February 13,2005)

During the apparitions, Mary asked the children: *"Do
you wish to offer yourselves to God to endure all the sufferings that He may be pleased to send you, as both an act of*

reparation for the sins with which He is offended and an act of supplication for the conversion of sinners?"

Lucia answered: *Yes, we do.*

Our Lady said: *"Well then, you will have much to suffer. But the grace of God will be your comfort."* Our Lady also told them: *"...Pray the Rosary every day in honor of Our Lady of the Rosary, in order to obtain peace for the world and the end of the war, for she alone can be of any avail... Sacrifice yourselves for sinners and say many times, especially when you make a sacrifice, 'O Jesus, this is for love of Thee, for the conversion of sinners, and in reparation for the sins committed against the Immaculate Heart of Mary.'"*

St. Jacinta said: **"If men knew the meaning of eternity, they would do anything to mend their lives." "I so love the Immaculate Heart of Mary!" "Her Heart is so good! How I love it!" "Sweet Heart of Mary, be my salvation!"** And also, **"The more I think the more I suffer, and I want to suffer for love of our Lord and for sinners."** At times, Jacinta kissed and embraced a crucifix exclaiming, **"O my Jesus! I love you and I want to suffer very much for Love of You."**

St. Francesco said, **"I would like to console our Lord, and after that convert sinners so that they won't offend Him anymore."**

<u>Ven. Antonetta Meo (December 15, 1930 – July 3, 1937)</u> was born December 15, 1930, in Rome, Italy. At age four she was diagnosed with advanced bone cancer and her leg was amputated at age five. During the evenings, her mother would read her the Catechism. During this time, she would also write letters to Jesus, Mary, and the saints. In total, she wrote over 100 letters. She placed these letters at the statue of baby Jesus in her room so that He could read them at night. In these letters she told Jesus that she had sinned. She also told Him that she offered herself to Him. The pain she endured, she offered to Jesus. In a letter she said that she gave her leg to Him. She said, **"The pain is like fabric, the stronger it is the more value it has."** She also said, "I want to stay with Him on the cross because I love Him". A few months before her First Holy Communion, Nennolina had written to Jesus:

"Dear Jesus Eucharist I love You so much! . . . Really very much! Not only because You are the Father of all the world, but also because You are the King of all the world, I always want to be Your lamp which burns night and day before You and near You in the Sacrament of the altar.

I'd like You to grant me three favors the first - make me saint, and this is the most important favor; the second - give me some souls; the third - make me walk normally, to tell the truth this is the least important. I'm not saying to give me back my leg, I gave it to You!

Dear Jesus I like my teacher Sister Noemi very much. I love her so, help her to do all the necessary things that You want her to do. Dear Jesus Eucharist! I love You so much so that I'm really longing for Christmas. Make my heart shine to You when You come into my poor heart. Dear Jesus, I'll make a lot of sacrifices that I'll offer to You when I do the First Holy Communion. Dear Jesus Eucharist! . . .I want to suffer a lot to redeem also the sins of men, especially of the very bad ones. Dear Jesus Eucharist I say good-bye to You and I kiss You. Your Antonietta. Good night Jesus good night Mary."

"Dear Jesus the Crucified, I love You so much. I love You so I want to stay with You on the Calvary and I suffer with joy because I know I'm on Calvary. Dear Jesus, I thank You for having sent me this illness because it is a means to get to Paradise. Dear Jesus tell God the Father that I love Him, too. Dear Jesus I want to be Your lamp and Your lily dear Jesus. Dear Jesus, give me the strength to bear this pain that I offer to You for sinners. Dear Jesus tell the Holy Spirit to enlighten me with love and fill me with its seven gifts. Dear Jesus tell sweet Virgin Mary that I love Her so much and I want to stay with Her on Calvary because I want to be Your victim of love dear Jesus. Dear Jesus, I entrust my father confessor to You and grant him every necessary favor. Dear Jesus I entrust my parents and my sister Margherita to You. Dear Jesus, greetings and kisses. – Antonietta of Jesus" (letter #162, written June 2, 1937 – a month before her death)

St. Jose Sanches del Rio (March 28, 1913 - February 10, 1928) was martyred in Mexico at the age of 14 and is the patron of persecuted Christians, children, and adolescents. At age 12, he wanted to join the Mexican Cristeros who were fighting against those killing Catholic priests and laity in Mexico. The general allowed him to become a flagbearer, and when he was captured (after having sacrificed his horse to the general so that he could escape), he refused to give up his faith. During his captivity, José was ordered to renounce his faith in Christ. Even under the threat of death, José refused. He was forced to watch the hanging of another Cristero. Instead of breaking his resolve, José encouraged the man, telling him they would meet again soon in Heaven.

During his time in captivity, José prayed the rosary daily and wrote a letter to his mother. He told her he was ready to fulfill the will of God. In an attempt to save him, José's father tried raising the funds for a ransom, but he was not able to do so in time. On February 10, 1928, after realizing they would not break José's faith, the government troops cut the bottom of his feet and forced him to walk around the town toward the cemetery. During his walk, José recited the rosary, prayed for his enemies, and sang songs to Our Lady of Guadalupe, despite being cut with a machete several times. He cried out in pain, but José did not give in. They told him if he shouted, "Death to Christ the King," they would spare his life. Instead, José would shout, *"I will never give in. Viva Cristo Rey y Santa Maria de Guadalupe!"* At the age of 14, St. José Luis Sánchez del Río died as a martyr on February 10, 1928.

St. Dominic Savio (April 2, 1842 - March 9, 1857) died at the age of 14 in 1857. Born and raised in Italy, Dominic showed signs of sanctity early on in life. When he was just 4 years old, Dominic was frequently found by his parents in solitary prayer. He learned to be an altar boy at age 5, and if he got to the church before the priest unlocked the doors in the morning, he would kneel (in the mud, snow, whatever) until the priest arrived. When he was just 7 years old, he wrote in his journal that he had four rules:

1) **I will go to Confession often, and as frequently to Holy Communion as my confessor allows.**
2) **I wish to sanctify the Sundays and festivals in a special manner.**
3) **My friends shall be Jesus and Mary.**
4) **Death rather than sin.**

He happened to attend the school of St. John Bosco, and John became a mentor for Dominic. As a pre-teen, he experimented with severe physical penances (putting rocks in his bed, wearing a hair shirt, etc.), but when his superiors found out, they forbade him from continuing them. Instead, he decided to simply perform all of his duties with as much love and humility as possible, which he summed up with the motto, *"I can't do big things but I want everything to be for the glory of God."* He contracted a lung disease and died soon after. After he died, John Bosco wrote a biography of Dominic, which was instrumental in Dominic being canonized.

<u>St. Maria Goretti (October 16, 1890 - July 06, 1902)</u> was the third of seven children in a poor farming family. When she was nine years old, her father died, leaving her family even more destitute. To survive, their family moved in with another family. During the day, most of Maria's siblings along with their mother would work the fields, while Maria would watch her baby sister, manage the house, and cook meals. It was a hard life, but they were devoted Christians and were close to one another.

One day when Maria was just 11 years old, the 20-year-old son of the family whose house they were sharing, Alessandro, came home early from his work when he knew that she would be alone (except for the infant she was watching). He had asked her to have sex with him twice before, and she had always refused. Wanting to rape her now, he brandished a knife and demanded that she submit to him. She refused, telling him that what he wanted to do was mortal sin, and warned him that he could go to hell for it. She fought him, screaming, *"No! It is a sin! God does not want it!"*

Furious, Alessandro first tried to choke her. When she continued to resist, he stabbed her 11 times. Injured badly but still alive, Maria tried to move toward the door. But he approached her again, stabbed her 3 more times, and then fled.

The baby woke up from the commotion and started crying. When Maria's mother and Alessandro's father came to check on the baby, they found Maria and rushed her to the hospital. She explained to her mother and the police what had happened, expressed forgiveness for Alessandro, and died soon after.

Alessandro was captured and sentenced to 30 years in prison. Though he was unrepentant for the first several years, he says that Maria visited him in a dream. Years later when he was released from prison, he apologized and sought forgiveness from Maria's mother, and received communion the next day. He said he would pray to Maria every day, calling her "his little saint." Amazingly, he attended Maria's canonization in 1950 and became a lay brother of the Order of Friars Minor Capuchin.

St. Vitus (290-303) was born at the end of the 3rd century
and was martyred at the beginning of the 4th century as a
child. Very little is known about his life. According to
legend, however, Vitus lived in a small town in Italy and
was a Christian while his father was a pagan. His father
tried to persuade him to leave the faith, but when he
refused, he ordered that Vitus be tortured. He survived the
torture and fled with his Christian tutors to Rome.
Unfortunately, Diocletian was the emperor. Vitus was
arrested and tortured again along with his tutors, but he
remained steadfast in the faith.

Before their torturers killed them, they were miraculously transported back to their home town and died there
of their wounds. Three days later, Vitus appeared in a

vision to a wealthy woman, who then found their bodies and buried them.

St. Rose of Viterbo (1233 - March 6, 1251) died when she was 18. Born around 1233, even as a small child Rose wanted to pray and help the poor. More than that, early on she displayed miraculous gifts. At the age of three, she apparently appeared to bring her aunt back from the dead. At the age of 7, she decided to live the life of a recluse, closed off from the world most of the time, engaged in prayer and penance. When she was 10, it is said that the Blessed Virgin Mary appeared to her and instructed her to enter the Third Order of St. Francis and to go preach in a nearby town. She entered the order, started wearing a habit, and would walk around town holding a crucifix, exhorting people to live a Christian life faithful to the Catholic Church.

When she was 15, she attempted to found a monastery, but failed. After that, she continued to live a recluse lifestyle, only infrequently going in public, and only to exhort people to penance. Two years later, her town erupted in revolt against the pope. Because she and her family supported the pope, they were exiled. Soon after, though, they were allowed to return.

When she heard that a nearby town was being oppressed by a sorceress, she visited and won the conversion of everyone in the town – including the sorceress. She did this by standing unharmed for 3 hours in a large fire. At the age of 18, she died of a heart condition. Rose's dying words to her parents were: **"I die with joy, for I desire to be united to my God. Live so as not to fear death. For those who live well in the world, death is not frightening, but sweet and precious."**

St. Agnes (291 – 304) was born to a noble Christian family in A.D. 291. She was a beautiful young girl and, combined with her noble background, had many suitors. She had intense devotion to her faith however, wished to remain a virgin for the kingdom of God, and showed little interest in the suitors. Offended, some of them reported to the Roman authorities that she was a Christian. Refusing to renounce her faith, a Roman official ordered that she be stripped naked and dragged through the streets to a brothel.

In one version of her story, her hair miraculously grew long and covered her body. At the brothel, any man who tried to rape her was immediately made blind. Undaunted, she was eventually tried in court and sentenced to death. Soldiers tied to her to stake, but when they lit the fire, she wouldn't burn. So, a Roman officer stabbed her with his sword, finally killing her.

Bl. Imelda Lambertini (1322 - May 12, 1333) (the patron saint of fervent First Communions) showed unusual piety even as a young child. She took great delight in prayer and would often slip off to a quiet corner of the house, which she adorned with flowers and pictures to make it a little oratory.

When she was nine, she was placed, at her own wish, in the Dominican convent in Val di Pietra to be trained there by the nuns. Her disposition soon endeared her to all, while the zeal with which she entered all the religious life of the house greatly edified the nuns. Her special devotion was to the Eucharistic presence of Our Lord at Mass and in the tabernacle. To receive Our Lord in Holy Communion became the consuming desire of her heart, but the custom of the place and time had fixed twelve as the earliest age for a first communion. She would sometimes exclaim: **"Tell me, can anyone receive Jesus into his heart and not die?"**

When she was eleven years old, she was present with the rest of the community at the Ascension Day Mass. All the others had received their communion: only Imelda was left unsatisfied. The nuns were preparing to leave the church when some of them were startled to see what appeared to be a Sacred Host hovering in the air above Imelda, as she knelt before the closed tabernacle absorbed in prayer. Quickly, they attracted the attention of the priest who hurried forward with a paten on which to receive It. In the face of such a miracle he could not do otherwise than give to Imelda her First Communion, which was also her last. For the rapture with which she received her Lord was so great that it broke her heart: she sank unconscious to the ground, and when loving hands upraised her, it was found that she was dead.

St. Tarcisius (3ʳᵈ Century) is another young saint, so fervent in his love for the Eucharist that he gave his life to protect it. Tarcisius was a twelve-year-old altar boy during one of the fierce Roman persecutions of the third century, probably during that of Valerian. Each day, from a secret meeting place in the catacombs where Christians gathered for Mass, a deacon would be sent to the prisons to carry the Eucharist to those Christians condemned to die. At one point, there was no deacon to send and so St. Tarcisius, an acolyte, was sent carrying the "Holy Mysteries" to those in prison.

On the way, he was stopped by boys his own age who were not Christians but knew him as a playmate and lover of games. He was asked to join their games, but this time he refused, and the crowd of boys noticed that he was carrying something. Somehow, he was also recognized as a Christian, and the small gang of boys, anxious to view the Christian "Mysteries," became a mob and turned upon Tarcisius with fury. He went down under the blows, and it is believed that a fellow Christian drove off the mob and rescued the young acolyte. The mangled body of Tarcisius was carried back to the catacombs, but the boy died on the way from his injuries. He was buried in the cemetery of St. Callistus, and his relics are claimed by the church of San Silvestro in Capite.

St. Stanislaw Kostka (October 28, 1550 - August 15, 1568) was born in 1550 in Rostków, a few kilometers from Warsaw. In 1564, when he was 14 years old, Stanislaus was sent to Vienna with his older brother to complete his studies with the Jesuits. He liked very much both his studies and the disciplined life of the college and already decided to enter the religious life. Unfortunately, the Jesuits had to close the college, and Stanislaus, his brother, and their tutor were forced to leave, eventually accepting the hospitality of a nobleman of the Lutheran faith. Stanislaus maintained his exemplary devotional lifestyle, despite the pressure from his brother, their tutor, and their host, all of whom criticized him for this. Stanislaus accepted all this with patience and submission, so much so that during the night, he prayed for them.

When he was about 17 years old, Stanislaus became gravely ill. We should point out that the young man belonged to the Confraternity of St. Barbara, whose members commend themselves to her as their patron to receive Holy Communion at the hour of death. Stanislaus, therefore, had complete trust that this would take place, and in fact awakened his tutor, who was keeping watch beside him, with the exclamation:

"Look, there is St. Barbara! Look, she has come with two Angels! She is bringing me the Blessed Sacrament!" And so it was: the Angels bent over him and gave him Holy Communion. The boy, now serene, lay down again on his bed. Several days later, to the surprise of all, Stanislaus got up, perfectly healed, stating that he wished to go to church to personally thank the Lord, and disclosing his wish to become a Jesuit.

The regional superior of the Jesuits refused him because of his young age and the lack of permission from his parents, but Stanislaus did not lose heart and decided at once to attempt to enter the Jesuits in Germany or even in Italy itself. He cast off his expensive clothing and dressed in that of a peasant, traveling on foot towards Augusta, where the great St. Peter Canisius, provincial of the Jesuits, was residing. When his brother discovered his absence, he searched for him for a long time and began to feel remorse for his hostile conduct towards him.

St. Peter Canisius carefully evaluated the young man's vocation, meanwhile, and decided to send him to the Jesuit seminary in Rome. In the letter of presentation for the young Stanislaus he wrote: *"Stanislaus, a noble son of Poland, a young man who is upright and full of zeal, was tested for a short time in the boarding house at Dillingen and was shown to be always diligent in fulfilling his duty and firm in his vocation...we expect great things from him."* However, Stanislaus did not complete his training. Nine months into his novitiate he again became very sick. Early in the morning on the feast of the Assumption, 1568, he told a priest that he saw Mary surrounded by many angels. And shortly afterward he died. Stanislaus was only seventeen years old when he "arrived in his own country to enjoy the vision of God."

Blessed Laura Vicuña (April 5, 1891 - January 22, 1904) was born on April 5, 1891, as the first child of a soldier who belonged to a noble Chilean family. A civil war broke out, and her father had to flee his country. A few days after the birth of the second child, her father died, leaving his wife and children alone. Seeing that she could not survive there, Laura's mother decided to leave the country. She finally found work at a large "hacienda" owned by a very questionable man in Argentina. Laura's mother let herself be won over by his promises of help and accepted his protection. She thought that his financial support would allow her to enroll her two girls as pupils in the Salesian Sisters' school nearby his hacienda.

Laura was very happy living under the serene guidance of the young Missionary Sisters. She discovered God, His love, and allowed herself to be surrounded by it. God's love stimulated her to love in return. Thus, Laura made herself available to all, helping them in any way she could. She was a leader and everyone's friend. But because of her deep religious interest, she was not well liked by her classmates. She spent most of her time praying in the school's chapel. She prayed every day for her mother's salvation and for her to leave the man she was with. Laura accepted God's love. Laura was fascinated by the ideal of the Sisters and secretly hoped to consecrate herself to God in the service of her brothers and sisters.

"I wish Mamma would know you better and be happy," she often prayed before the tabernacle. Laura was distressed about her mother's situation with the owner of the hacienda; her mother was indeed far away from God, and he was the cause. The struggle for living and providing for her daughters had wearied her. In a moment of stress and discouragement, she had given in to his demands. During one of her school vacations, Laura herself was even beaten twice by this man, who wanted her to forget about becoming a nun. She held to this desire even when he stopped paying for her education, and when the nuns at her school learned of the conflict, they gave Laura and her sister scholarships. Although she was grateful to her teachers, she still worried about her mother's situation. One day, remembering the phrase of Jesus: *"No one has greater love than to give up one's life for one's friends,"* Laura decided to give her life in exchange for her mother's salvation. Laura, believing that her love of God and of her mother was stronger than death, said to the Lord: **"I offer you my life for that of my mother."** As time passed, she became seriously ill with pulmonary tuberculosis.

The winter of 1903 in their home was extremely severe, with persistent rain and dampness. Laura became weaker with each passing day; she was wasting away. Although her mother took her to where the climate was more pleasant and helpful, there was no improvement in her health. Laura knew she would not recover. God had accepted her offering... her self-immolation. Laura's mother remained day and night at her bedside, surrounding her with care and attention. Laura kept looking at her tenderly. Now it was time to reveal her secret. **"Mamma, I'm dying, but I'm happy to offer my life for you. I asked Our Lord for this. Before I die, Mother, would I have the joy of seeing you repent?"** Her mother was shocked. She fell on her knees sobbing. She instantly understood everything. Her mother, crying, answered: *"I swear, I will do whatever you ask me! God is the witness of my promise! Laura, my daughter, please forgive me... O dear God, please forgive my life of sin... Yes, I will start again."* Laura smiled and said: **"Thank you, Jesus! Thank you, Mary! Goodbye, Mother! Now I die happy!"** On January 22, 1904, Laura died of her disease, weakened by the physical abuse she previously received from the owner of the hacienda, having offered her life for the salvation of her mother. One of Laura's famous sayings was **"Suffer silently and Smile always."**

Blessed Carlo Acutis (May 3, 1991 - Oct 12, 2006) was born May 3, 1991, in London, where his parents were working. Just a few months later, his parents moved to Milan. As a small child, a Polish nanny helped to take care of Carlo and not only taught him catechism, but also instilled in him a deep love for the Eucharist, Mass, and the

Rosary. Even as a small child he attended daily Mass and prayed the daily rosary.

Carlo was very proficient with computer programming and designed several websites to evangelize about the faith – most well-known was his website about Eucharistic Miracles. As a teenager, Carlo was diagnosed with leukemia. He offered his sufferings for Pope Benedict XVI and for the Church, saying **"I offer all the suffering I will have to suffer for the Lord, for the Pope, and the Church."** He died on Oct. 12, 2006, and was buried in Assisi, at his request, because of his love for St. Francis of Assisi. His cause for canonization began in 2013. He was designated "Venerable" in 2018 and designated "Blessed" October 10, 2020. Some of his most well-known sayings were:

"Always to be united with Jesus, this is my program of life."

"The more we receive the Eucharist, the more we will become like Jesus, so that on this earth we will have a foretaste of heaven."

"Everything passes away ... What alone will truly make us beautiful in God's eyes is the way that we have loved him and our brothers."

"The Virgin Mother is the only woman in my life ... I never fail to keep the most gracious appointment of the day – recitation of the Holy Rosary."

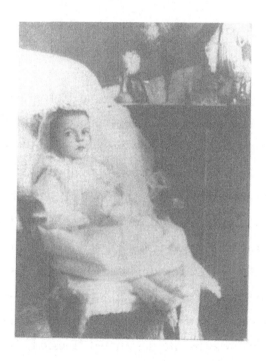

Little Nellie of Holy God (Nellie Organ August 24, 1903 - February 2, 1908) is not a canonized saint, although her life is such a witness of holiness in a child and had such an impact upon the Church (in an indirect way) that I felt compelled to add a little bit about her. About two years after her death, Pope St Pius X heard this child's story and exclaimed, *"There! That is the sign for which I was waiting."* A few months later in 1910 he issued *"Quam Singulari,"* which significantly lowered the age of Holy Communion for children.

Little Nellie only lived to be four and a half years old, yet she is called "The Little Violet of the Blessed Sacrament." Nellie was born in Ireland, the youngest of four children. *"When only two,"* Nellie's father writes, *"she would clasp my hand and toddle off to Mass, prattling all the way about Holy God. That was the way she always spoke of God, and I do not know where she could have learned it."* The holy Names of Jesus and Mary were her first words, and she loved to pray the rosary with her family every night. Her father was a soldier, and when her mother died of tuberculosis when Nellie was four years old her father entrusted her and her sister to the Good Shepherd Sisters. Nellie had been dropped as a baby and so always had problems with her spine (and walking) and eventually herself became ill with tuberculosis, from which she died a few months later.

Nellie had a great devotion to the Child Jesus and an innate love of His Presence in the Blessed Sacrament. She experienced several visions of the Christ Child, but more than all else she longed to receive Him in the Blessed Sacrament.

One day, the Sisters mentioned to a visiting priest the longing for Holy Communion of the "extraordinary child" upstairs. Nellie was only 4 years old, and at this time children generally were not admitted to Holy Communion until ten or twelve years of age. This priest, Father Bury, far from dismissing the Sisters' account, gave his sympathetic attention. "St. Alphonsus," he said, "gave Holy Communion to a tiny child who longed for it. If the Bishop permitted me, I would do the same by Little Nellie." So that day Fr. Bury went up and had a talk with Nellie. "What is the Blessed Eucharist?" he asked. Nellie's reply was all her own: there was not a touch of coaching or catechism about it. **"It is Holy God,"** she lisped; **"it is Him that makes the nuns and everybody else holy."** On another occasion she would say, **"Jesus comes on my tongue and goes down into my heart."** The words were indeed the words of an infant, but the doctrine was profound.

Impressed by the reasoning of Nellie, Father Bury wrote a letter to the Bishop requesting special permission to give her Holy Communion. According to Father Bury, *"With regard to the reception of this Sacrament, Nellie had arrived at the use of reason."* He told the Bishop that Nellie was endowed in no ordinary degree with ardent love of God and the desire to be united to Him in Holy Communion.

The Bishop granted permission. When Nellie heard the news, her joy was indescribable. **"I will have Holy God in my heart!!! I will have Holy God in my heart!"** she kept repeating with indescribable joy! Nellie could hardly sleep the night before her First Holy Communion. Those present were struck by her devotion and love. A priest wrote in October, 1911, describing Nellie's thanksgiving after her First Communion. *"The happy moment will long be remembered by those who had the privilege of being present. Nellie seemed in an ecstasy, and all remarked the heavenly light that lighted up the child's countenance."*

Nellie also had a great love for Jesus crucified. She kept a crucifix beside her on her bed, and when her sufferings became almost unbearable, she would take it in her little hand, stare at it fixedly, and whisper, **"Poor Holy God! Oh, poor Holy God!"** If others sympathized with her, she would smile and remark, **"What is it compared with what He suffered on the Cross for me?"**

On the day that Nellie was to die, toward three o'clock she became quite calm and remained motionless for about an hour. Her eyes were fixed on something which she seemed to see at the foot of her bed. *"There was an extraordinary look in those lovely eyes,"* a Sister related; *"it was not the sightless, glazed expression of the dying."* Then Nellie moved. Her eyes now filled with tears - with tears of joy, it seemed. She tried to rise and draw near to that "something" on which she was gazing so longingly, and then she smiled. From the movement of her lips, it seemed she was speaking with someone, and raising her eyes, she followed with a look of supernatural love that "something," which seemed now to hover above her head. Presently, with an ecstatic smile, little Nellie "flew" to Holy God. It was four o'clock on Sunday, February 2, 1908, the Feast of the Purification of Mary and of the Presentation of the Child Jesus in the Temple (Candlemas Day). Nellie was then four years, five months, and eight days old.

Exactly a year and a week after little Nellie's death, the grave was opened to see if a transference of her body could be safely accomplished. The Reverend Dr. Scannell will now tell us what took place at the exhumation:

"There were present a priest (this was Fr. Scannell himself), the Nurse, and two other reliable witnesses. To the great astonishment of all, for it must be borne in mind that the child had died of phthisis (a wasting or consumption of the tissue; usually, pulmonary tuberculosis) the body was found. intact, except for a small cavity in the right jaw which corresponded to the bone that had been destroyed by caries whilst the little one was still alive. The fingers were quite flexible and the hair had grown a little. The dress, the wreath and veil of First Communion, with which she had been buried as she desired, were still intact. The silver medal of the saintly child of Mary was bright as if it had been recently

polished; everything, in fact, was found to be exactly as on the day of Nellie's death."

<u>Servant of God Charlene Marie Richard (January 13, 1947 – August 11, 1959)</u> is a child on her way to canonization who is particularly close to me, although I only recently learned of her. First of all, we share a birthday (January 13th), and she also is American – a Catholic Cajun girl from Richard, Louisiana. She also is close to my heart as she eventually died from acute lymphatic leukemia – and blood cancers (lymphoma and chronic leukemia) run in my family (several of my siblings have battled these).

Charlene was a normal child no more devoted to God than others of her age. But in May 1959, after reading a book about Therese of Lisieux, Charlene asked her grandmother whether she, too, could become a saint by praying like Therese. She started reporting appearances of a tall woman in black who would appear and disappear in front of her eyes, and her teachers said that she wasn't herself, so her parents took her to a doctor. Just two weeks before she died, she was diagnosed with cancer. Her parents asked the hospital chaplain to inform her of her upcoming death, and Charlene accepted all with great resignation to the will of God. Though the illness was painful, she remained cheerful, meekly accepted her fate, and offered up her suffering to God. The priest who visited her daily, as well as a sister at the hospital, attested to her deep spirituality and devotion. She offered her sufferings for the conversion of souls and the Church. Often when the priest recommended someone to her prayers, he would see miraculous results. Charlene looked forward to his visits daily, and when he came into the room, she would say to the visiting priest full of cheerfulness, **"OK, Father, who am I to suffer for today?"**

Sister M. Theresita Crowley was the pediatric supervisor at the time Charlene entered Our Lady of Lourdes hospital in Lafayette. She remembers Charlene as a pious little girl. *"Charlene suffered a great deal; it's the nature of the disease. The pain is awful and there is almost constant bleeding and hemorrhage but I remember her as a cheerful patient. She never complained."* She continues, *"Of all the beautiful, sick children I have tended to in my career as a nurse, Charlene stands out in a very special way. I learned a lot from Charlene, especially from her willingness to accept everything. Her life was full in a short span."*

One of the sisters at the hospital said that she remembers that Charlene was especially fearful of the bone marrow tests which involved inserting a long needle through the breast bone. *"I held her hand through the entire procedure,"* Sister said. *"I suggested to her that we make it a big prayer. Charlene's prayer was that one of her brothers become a priest. She was very zealous to have a brother-priest."* Charlene's prayer for a brother-priest was not answered directly. While one brother, John Dale, did enter Immaculata Seminary for a short while, he eventually became a licensed practical nurse and married. But Charlene lacks no brothers numbered among the priesthood, for it seems to be the priests in the diocese, especially in the area around where she lived and died, who have the most confidence in her, who openly express their belief in her sainthood and who encourage others to pray to her for intercession with God in times of need. Many priests have received miraculous answers to prayers through the intercession of little Charlene.

Dr. Voorhies was a friend of the chaplain who daily visited Charlene. He went to check on Charlene at 2:30 am on the morning of August 11 and said that *"she was in considerable pain"*. He later recalled he was very concerned about Charlene's condition, so much so that he began his rounds earlier that morning. He said, *"When I went to her room she was alone and there was evidence of extensive bleeding, I was incensed that a nurse had left a patient alone."*

Charlene died at 7:20 am on the morning of August 11, 1959, approximately 13 hours after Dr. Voorhies discovered her alone and bleeding.

Father Joseph Brennen – Charlene's chaplain – said, *"She was a faith-filled little girl. I see Charlene as a witness for all people of all ages to the power of resignation and acceptance of God's will. She wasn't different in any way except that when crisis came in her life (and it came very early), she accepted it with faith, trust and love".*

Bl. Rolando Rivi (January 7, 1931 – April 13, 1945) was a 14-year-old Italian seminarian from Italy, who died as a martyr in a little town called Monchio, in the province of Modena. He began serving Mass at the age of five, and on the feast of Corpus Christi, June 16, 1938 he made his first Communion. Confirmed in 1940 at the age of nine, Rolando declared an early desire to become **"a perfect Christian and a soldier for Jesus Christ."** At age 11, he was enrolled in the minor seminary and clothed in a cassock and wore a staturno as was the customary clerical dress.

Many times, he said that the cassock was a sign **"that I belong to Jesus."** He was known to be an excellent student, with deep and serious religious devotion. He wanted to become a missionary, and he was known to have great musical talent. He was always encouraging his fellow students and friends to come to Mass, to pray the rosary, and his grandma noted that his passion for life would surely make him end up being either *"a saint or a scoundrel."*

In the summer of 1944, his seminary was occupied by German troops. Rolando moved home but continued to wear his cassock and to study under the tutelage of his parish priest. **"I study to be a priest, and these vestments are the sign that I belong to Jesus,"** Rolando told those, including his parents, who were worried that his public witness would mean danger. This was a little dangerous, since nearly 100 priests had been killed the previous year by Communist partisans. On April 10, 1945, a group of these partisans kidnapped Rolando as he was studying in a little grove near his home. His parents discovered both his books and a note from the partisans warning them not to look for him. He was taken to a farmhouse, beaten and tortured for three days, under the absurd accusation that he had been a spy for the Germans; he was then dragged into the woods, stripped of his cassock, and shot twice in the head. The communists killed him, even though he was only 14 years old, because, as one killer put it, it would mean "one less future priest." The partisans rolled his cassock up into a ball and used it to play soccer. His father and parish priest discovered his body the following day.

The decree recognizing that Rolando's violent death was inflicted "in odium fidei" was signed by the Pope on March 28, 2013, and his beatification as a martyr was celebrated on October 5th of that year. On his tomb is written **"Io sono di Gesù,"** Italian for **"I belong to Jesus."** Rolando is a powerful intercessor not only for persecuted Christians, but also for seminarians and priests struggling with or suffering within their vocation.

St Pedro Calungsod (July 21, 1654 - April 02, 1672) is a Filipino Roman Catholic martyr who was killed while doing missionary work in Guam in 1672. At 14 years old, he volunteered to go and help in the missions. The life was brutal, often walking hours barefoot through jungles, rowing boats for hours to take the missionaries to their missions, and often sleeping in the grass under the sky. Pedro was a sacristan and teacher of catechism alongside the Spanish Jesuit missionary Blessed Diego Luis de San Vitores, and through their efforts countless people received the sacraments, especially that of Baptism. When a Chinese man began to falsely accuse the missionaries of spreading poison through the ritual of the pouring of water (i.e., baptism), and through the ritual of Catholic Masses, a plot

developed to kill them. Pedro Calungsod and Diego San
Vitores were both murdered after baptizing an infant and
mother who converted to the Roman Catholic faith. In his
book *Pedro Calungsod: Young Visayan Protomartyr*, Fr.
Catalino G. Arevalo, S.J., wrote a fascinating account of
Pedro Calungsod's martyrdom at the hands of two enraged
pagan natives named Matapang and Hurao on April 2,
1672:

> *The two would-be killers come to him first, so he
> cannot protect the priest, and throw spears and darts in
> his direction. Pedro dodges them, running from the
> attackers, but not so as to abandon the priest...A spear
> finally pierces his chest. He falls mortally wounded. One
> of the killers runs to him, and splits his skill with a
> machete. San Vitores, seeing Pedro fall, rushes towards
> him...he says some words to the dying Pedro, and blesses
> him with his crucifix.*
>
> *Then the Jesuit turns to Matapang and Hurao,
> raising the crucifix before their eyes, urging them to yield
> themselves even now to the Christ who died for them on
> the Cross...A spear finds Diego Luis' breast also, and as
> the priest staggers, the two killers come nearer...he falls
> to the earth beside Pedro's bloodied body...*
>
> *Then Matapang and Hurao bind the two bodies
> together, attach a large rock to their feet. They place
> them quickly in a banca, and row out with them to the*

sea. They throw the two still bodies, of the indefatigable Spanish missionary and his faithful catechist and lay helper, into the deep waters.

The love of Christ that led Pedro to embrace such a difficult mission at such a young age was the same Love that held him faithful as a witness to Jesus even through a brutal death.

Bl. Chiara Luce Badano (October 29, 1971 - October 7, 1990) was born in a quiet, mountain town in Italy. She was described by her mother, Maria Teresa Badano, thus: **"Chiara had many toys and like all children she liked to play. One day, while she was playing in her room and I**

was working in the kitchen, I told Chiara: "Surely, you have many toys, lots of them!" She replied: "Yes, why?" I said: "Couldn't you give some to the poor?" She answered: "They are mine!" And she grabs her toys out of fear. After some time, while I am in the kitchen, I hear her say: "This one yes, this one no...!" I was curious, I looked from her door and saw that she had divided all her toys and then she told me: "Bring me a bag mum," I brought her the bag and she put some of her toys into it. I asked her: "But Chiara, these are the new ones!" And she said: "Mum, I cannot give old and broken toys to poor children."

When Chiara was nine years old, the Badano family traveled to Rome for a "Family Fest." There, the Focolare Movement helped Chiara encounter Christ's love in a new light. After the event, Chiara began making friends with the youth of the Focolare Movement. Regarding her enthusiasm for the faith, Chiara wrote, "**I have rediscovered the Gospel ... I was not an authentic Christian because I did not live it fully. I won't and cannot remain illiterate of such an extraordinary message. Now I want to make this wonderful book the only goal of my life.**"

When Chiara was seventeen, she was taken to the hospital for acute shoulder pain experienced during a tennis match. She then received the diagnosis of bone cancer (osteogenic sarcoma with metastases). Chiara was initially devastated by her illness, but quickly learned how to say "yes" to Jesus in the midst of her greatest suffering.

At the beginning of chemotherapy, Chiara lost use of her legs. She wrote, "**I felt so little. The path seemed so hard. I often felt oppressed by the pain, and I used to repeat: 'For you, Jesus: if you want this, so do I!'**" When she lost the use of her legs, Chiara Luce said, "**If I had to choose between walking or going to heaven, I would choose going to heaven.**" With the last CAT scan, all hopes of remission disappeared. Chiara's smile and attentive love never ceased. Her family would even catch her singing while she was alone. Chiara's friends who visited her in the hospital said, "*At first we thought we would visit Chiara to keep her spirits up, however, we soon realized that in fact, we were the ones who needed her. Her life was like a magnet drawing us towards her.*"

On July 19, 1989, Chiara Luce nearly died because of a hemorrhage. She said to her mother Teresa: "**Don't shed any tears for me. I'm going to Jesus. At my funeral, I don't want people crying, but singing with all their hearts.**" She wrote to her friends, "**Previously I felt another world was awaiting me and the most I could do was to let go. Instead now I feel enfolded in a marvelous plan of God which is slowly being unveiled to me.**" She confided: "**I no longer ask Jesus to come and take me away to heaven. I don't want to give him the impression that I don't want to suffer any longer**". She knew what lay before her and she did not want to change anything (she did not pray for a cure but to be able to do God's will).

Speaking of this all she said, **"I suffered a lot, but my soul was singing."** Towards the end of her illness she said, **"I have nothing left, but I still have my heart. And with that I can always love."**

Chiara was in much pain before she died, but she refused morphine, saying **"It will take away my lucidity and I can only offer Jesus my pain."**

Together with her mother, Chiara Luce prepared for her funeral, which she wanted to be a 'wedding ceremony'. She chose how she wanted to be dressed, what songs would be sung, the flowers and the Mass readings. She told her mother, **"When you're getting me ready, Mum, you have to keep saying to yourself, 'Chiara Luce is now seeing Jesus."** At the moment she died, her parents were at her bedside and all of her friends were nearby in an adjoining room. There was a great sense of peace. Chiara's last words to her mother Teresa were: **"Goodbye. Be happy because I'm happy."**

Section Two

Spiritual Formation of Children

Formation of Love
Baptism and the Sacraments
A Child's Name
Preserving Baptismal Grace
Developing a Child's Natural Virtue
Spiritual Direction
Catechesis
Listening to God
Teaching Active Virtue

Chapter 6

Spiritual Formation of Children

Formation of Love

The first 'concept' of God that a child has in his or her mind comes through parental love. A small child cannot 'understand' God or 'know' Him in his or her mind except through the image and idea he or she receives modeled by his or her parents. Of course, the soul of a child 'knows' God instinctively and shares a love relationship with Him – even a quite deep one. But a child's understanding of God begins with the face of his or her own mother and father.

Every person's identity stems from his or her creation by God for the purpose of living as a child of God while on earth and then forever with God in eternity. This base truth of each soul's purpose and identity as a child of God must be taught to him/her from the get-go. From the very first moments that a parent is conscience of the new baby's existence within his or her mother's womb, the parent should start helping the child to build a self-understanding of being a child of God. In the beginning, this is done primarily through the love the parents pour out on that child (which the child can spiritually sense, even while still in his/her mother's womb) and through the prayer poured over them by his/her parents. Simply by telling the tiny, unborn baby how loved he or she is – or by praying aloud together (a rosary, for example) – the parents are surrounding their little one with such an atmosphere of grace that it gives new, strong life to the baby's heart and soul, just as much as the mother is physically nourishing his/her body.

The first and most fundamental truth about the human person that a child needs to know through experience from the very moment of their conception is that every soul is created in love by God for love, for God. I say that this is experiential knowledge because it is simply through one's creation and very existence that one begins to experience this truth firsthand. Without the Breath of God breathing life – a soul – into a combination of cells created by the union of a man's sperm and a woman's egg, life wouldn't exist. The ultimate Giver of all Life is God. The ultimate Sustainer of all Life is God. And the ultimate Taker of all Life back into eternity with Him through death is God. This is a fundamental truth that spans way beyond one's simple religious beliefs – it is something that can be proven through the scientific order.

It is so important for a child – or any human person for that matter – to really understand that they were created in Love, for Love. Without the 'instructions' of God's Love written on the human heart, a person would have no idea how or why he was brought into existence. And it is this purpose of being created BY LOVE and FOR LOVE that will eventually shape every choice he has to make as he develops into an adult.

A child's first 'concept' of God comes to him through his parents. His understanding of being created by Love and for Love is something that he comes to know simply because he is loved and taught to love by those to whom he is entrusted, namely his parents. It is important for any child's development into a healthy adult that they really experience this truth in some way from the youngest moments of their lives – it is from this experience of being created by Love and for Love that they build a self-understanding of being a child of God from the very moment of their conception. Because of original sin, Baptism is the necessary 'medicine' needed to reclaim, rewash, reform a little soul stained by it back into his childhood in the bosom of God. But the purpose of his existence – to live as an authentic child of God – is present in the mind and desires of God's heart from the very get-go... from that first beat of his little heart under the breast of his mother.

Baptism and the Sacraments

The most important gift that a parent can give to a child is the gift of Baptism. In Baptism, a person is made into a son or daughter of God. By making their child into a child of God, parents are giving him/her access to all the special graces and 'rights' of such a child. He/she will be bestowed with whatever is necessary to fulfill the will of our heavenly Father, which in turn, will give him/her true happiness.

There are two important considerations for parents to discern concerning their child's Baptism: the name that the child will be given, as well as the godparents chosen to witness the Baptism and ensure that the child is raised in the Catholic faith (if something were to prevent the parents from doing that in the future.) Neither of these two choices (that of a baptismal name and of godparents) is arbitrary. Names are important and parents should really put the question to prayer as they try to discern what name God might desire for their little one.

A Child's Name

When we reflect on the importance of the name given to a child, the most obvious example to look to is that of Jesus Christ Himself – the 'Anointed Savior' was specifically given the name of Jesus and was also called 'Emmanuel – 'God with us."

"His name shall be Emmanuel, 'God is with us.'" – Isaiah 7:14

"Joseph, son of David, do not fear to take Mary your wife, for that which is conceived in her is of the Holy Spirit; she will bear a son, and you shall call his name Jesus, for he will save his people from their sins.'" –Mt 1:20-21

It's clear from these passages that Jesus' Name has importance – and this is because names have a meaning.

Jesus' very name means that God is with us – and that has power. It is for this reason that *'at the Name of Jesus, every knee shall bend, in heaven and on earth and under the earth..."* (Phil 2:10)

Many other Biblical figures also had names of importance, and each child born on earth should be given a name of importance. The importance of names can be seen way back in Genesis from the beginning when God created the world. When Adam was alone in the Garden of Eden, God brought each of the animals to him *to name*. And once Eve was created from his side, she was presented to him by God, and he said: *"This one at last is bone of my bones and flesh of my flesh. **She shall be called Woman, because she taken out of Man.'"** –*Genesis 2:23 And later on: **"The man called his wife's name Eve, because she was the mother of all the living.**" Gen 3:20

Later on in Genesis, God appeared to Abram and changed his name to Abraham. He appeared to Jacob and changed his name to Israel. In the Gospels, Jesus changed Cephas' name to Peter, and in the book of Acts, Saul's name was changed to Paul.

Perhaps, after Jesus, no other name is so revered and full of power as that of Our Lady – Mary, Miriam. On September 12th we celebrate the Feast of the Name of Mary. The history of the Blessed Mother's name is multifaceted. Some translations say it means, *"wished for child"* (a child not only 'wished for' by Anna and Joachim, but by all of humanity). Mary longed for the Messiah, but Israel longed for Her to give the Messiah. The Latin translation of Mary from the Hebrew means, _"Sea, Star, "Drop of the Sea"_. St. Jerome (writing c. 390), following Eusebius of Caesarea, translates the name as "drop of the sea" (_stella maris_ in <u>Latin</u>), from Hebrew מר _mar_ "drop" (cf. Isaias 40:15) and ים _yam_ "sea" This translation was subsequently rendered _stella maris_ ("<u>star of the sea</u>") due to scribal error, whence <u>Our Lady</u>'s title <u>Star of the Sea</u>. Both reflect her identity – both as the sea of love that quench's Jesus' thirst and the sea that we travel to reach heaven (for She is the one who gave us Jesus who opened the gates of heaven to us for eternity). Mary is also our star, lighting the way in earth's darkness pointing the way to Christ. In Egyptian, Mary means "<u>Beloved.</u>" And in Hebrew, it means "<u>Bitterness</u>", while others translate it "<u>rebelliousness.</u>" It is beautiful to think of how Our Lady took all bitterness of the Cross and made it all sweet for Jesus. And it was Mary who CRUSHED ALL REBELLIOUSNESS WITH FIAT!

As we see that Mary was given her name for all these reasons, it causes us to reflect on what it means to name a child. Names mean things. Through bestowing a name at birth and at Baptism, a parent is blessing a child through that name. It is creative. If you name your child a Christian name, you are not only influencing his or her character (if you name a child 'strength of God,' you are not only bestowing that gift/grace on him or her every time you call his or her name), but you are also giving him or her protectors (of saints) to overshadow his or her life as well. The *Catechism of the Catholic Church* says regarding the name given to a child:

> *2156 The sacrament of Baptism is conferred "in the name of the Father and of the Son and of the Holy Spirit." (Mt 28:19) In Baptism, the Lord's name sanctifies man, and the Christian receives his name in the Church. This can be the name of a saint, that is, of a disciple who has lived a life of exemplary fidelity to the Lord. The patron saint provides a model of charity; we are assured of his intercession. The "baptismal name" can also express a Christian mystery or Christian virtue. "Parents, sponsors, and the pastor are to see that a name is not given which is foreign to Christian sentiment." (Code of Canon Law 855)*
>
> *2157 The Christian begins his day, his prayers, and his activities with the Sign of the Cross: "in the name of the Father and of the Son and of the Holy Spirit. Amen." The baptized person dedicates the day to the glory of God and calls on the Savior's grace which lets him act in the Spirit as a child of the Father. The sign of the cross strengthens us in temptations and difficulties.*
>
> *2158 God calls each one by name. (Is 43:1 and Jn 10:3) Everyone's name is sacred. The name is the icon of*

the person. It demands respect as a sign of the dignity of the one who bears it.

2159 The name one receives is a name for eternity. In the kingdom, the mysterious and unique character of each person marked with God's name will shine forth in splendor. "To him who conquers . . . I will give a white stone, with a new name written on the stone which no one knows except him who receives it." (Rev 2:17) "Then I looked, and Lo, on Mount Zion stood the Lamb, and with him a hundred and forty-four thousand who had his name and his Father's name written on their foreheads." (Rev 14:1)

The Gift of Godparents

The gift of who a parent invites to be a child's godparent is also something that should be prayed about long and hard. A child's godparent must be someone who will aid that child in faith – first and foremost by praying regularly for him/her, as well as in setting a positive example for him/her through their own Christian witness of life. Holy godparents have a great spiritual authority over a growing child – and their prayers before God on behalf of that child have a special weight simply because they accepted the call to be godparents.

Preserving Baptismal Grace

One more little aspect of Baptism that I would like to mention before we move on is the importance of helping children to preserve the purity of their Baptismal grace. When a person is baptized, the Church presents them with a white garment and says 'bring this garment undirtied with you into heaven...' The godparents can help the parents and other family members to protect a child's innocence and to teach them right from wrong, how to form lives of virtue, so that when they die one day they may still be clad spiritually in the white Baptismal grace. This will not only be a gift at the end of their lives, but through keeping such Baptismal purity unsullied, the child will be an example of Christ to others in the world... hence the Church gifts a child with a baptismal candle declaring the child to be a witness of Christ's light. Godparents can help a child's light grow ever brighter and stronger as they grow in age. Lastly, a child's lips, head, heart, eyes, and ears are anointed with sacred chrism. This is so that their words, thoughts, desires, and loves, what they see and what they hear may all be instruments to bring God's love more greatly into the world.

Once children reach the age of reason, they should be taught to go to Confession after they sin to keep their hearts in a state of grace. But children should also be taught preventative measures that help to keep their hearts in a state of grace (before falling into sin). Virtue is learned and developed. And so, parents (and other family members and godparents) must not allow a child's soul to grow uncultivated, but instead work hard day in and day out to not only set good examples for a child, but also to teach the child how to develop virtue in little ways throughout the day. Homes must be kept as places that treasure virtue –with an atmosphere of purity – free from evil words, evil images and most of all, evil actions.

Developing a Child's Natural Virtue

Children have natural spiritual gifts that form a solid foundation on which God can easily build strong lives of virtue. Some of these spiritual gifts are littleness and humility, forgiveness, docility, purity, and trust. It is so important for a parent to preserve these God given gifts and to build on them. Jesus Himself recognized these gifts, not only confirming them but also holding them out as examples for adults to emulate if they, too, wanted to reach heaven.

"Then children were brought to him that he might lay his hands on them and pray. The disciples rebuked them, but Jesus said, "Let the children come to me, and

*do not prevent them; for the kingdom of heaven belongs to such as these." After he placed his hands on them, he went away." –*Matthew 19:13-15

*"At that time the disciples approached Jesus and said, "Who is the greatest in the kingdom of heaven?" He called a child over, placed it in their midst, and said, "Amen, I say to you, unless you turn and become like children, you will not enter the kingdom of heaven. Whoever humbles himself like this child is the greatest in the kingdom of heaven. And whoever receives one child such as this in my name receives me." –*Matthew 18:1-5

Why would the Lord say these words? It is because children are created with a natural holiness; you could say – a natural purity that comes from the simple fact that they are innocent babies fresh from the hands and heart of the Father. These natural gifts that come through littleness are the foundation blocks that grace can build on to strengthen a child in his or her sonship and daughterhood claimed by the Father in Baptism. What are the natural gifts of a small child and makes one automatically think about purity and holiness, even when one's mind is far from religion?

Littleness: Psalm 131: *"LORD, my heart is not proud; nor are my eyes haughty. I do not busy myself with great matters, with things too sublime for me. Rather, I have stilled my soul, Like a weaned child to its mother, weaned is my soul. Israel, hope in the LORD, now and forever."* Little souls are humble souls. When one is little, one naturally depends on others and naturally trusts. In being little (empty of oneself and open to receive God's gifts), God's omnipotence can work fully through their souls. In littleness, a soul only has what his Father thinks is good to offer to him.

Purity: A child is naturally pure. Purity means to be without sin, without stain or dirt – to be without obstacles blocking the natural goodness and light God places within one's soul from shining through. Purity regards body – only using it for the purpose for which God created it. Purity regards the mind – only thinking about holy things, things that elevate one's soul to God, to love. Purity regards intention – it is empty of vanity and ambition and desires solely goodness for the other. Purity in itself is so clear that it doesn't even consider things that are sinful, hurtful, or disordered. Purity is necessary for God's pure love to pour through one's soul. And more than being a lack of sinful or evil things, true purity means simply being full of the presence of God. A pure mind thinks of God – a pure mouth speaks of God – pure eyes look to God – a pure body works for God.

Docility: When you look at a child's body, you see a strong manifestation of his or her docility. But the vulnerability, formability, and fragility, so to say, of a child goes beyond their weak, little body incapable of even holding their own head up – their mind is vulnerable and impressionable – their heart beats only of love. This docility is a gift when a child is taught to conform their docile will to God's will and to allow God to be their strength.

Trust: A child automatically trusts – it is not something that a child does because of reason and will; instead, children have an innate trust that pervades the way they interact with the people and world around them. Children should be taught through their trust of their parents that their needs will be met. Responding to a child's cries teaches the child to trust the responder. And such trust can be transferred to the spiritual life quite easily when a child has a good foundation of human trust in their family. It is easier for children to trust God if they can trust the people around them.

Forgiveness: A child doesn't even know that he is forgiving when he is forgiving. A child's memory simply doesn't really remember or dwell on the faults of people around

him or her – even when he or she is affected by them nega-
tively. A child simply beams of love at all who surround
him or her. And a child's forgiveness is infectious.

Wonder and Awe: A child naturally is struck with great
wonder and awe at everything God 'surprises' him or her
with in creation. A butterfly that you and I might pass by
can be the object of a child's attention for hours – watching
it, drawing it, imitating it, talking about it, sometimes even
catching it. A child's wonder and awe teach adults to not
take God's gifts for granted.

Simplicity: A child naturally takes everything in this
complicated world around him or her and makes it simple.
It's the guilelessness and simplicity of a child's thinking,
speaking, and interacting with others that so strongly at-
tracts the Heart of God to himself.

Senses and Children – Innocence is preserved by the
presence of God; When what children see, hear, and experience is total purity, then their hearts are total purity.
Children are formed soaked in the presence of God – they
literally come from heaven. It is a parent's job to keep this
atmosphere of God and His Love always around a child so
that they can be preserved in purity in all of their senses.

"Whoever causes one of these little ones who believe in me to sin, it would be better for him to have a great millstone hung around his neck and to be drowned in the depths of the sea." Matthew 18:5

Such are the basic building blocks of a child's spiritual formation in God from the time of his or her earliest existence: children are surrounded by Love, given a name, baptized, and encouraged to develop their natural virtue. Once a child begins to grow a little, he or she begins to relate to the world not just by love, but also by imagination and reason. And so begins the parent's responsibility to fill these growing places of a child's mind and heart with right thinking, helping him/her to *'put on the mind of Christ.'* (1 Cor 2:16) How to do this we will address in the next chapter.

Chapter 7

Spiritual Direction for Children

Catechesis

The foundation block of spiritual direction for children is the teaching of basic catechetical truths to them from the earliest of ages. As an infant in arms, children begin to learn to know and love God and to communicate with Him in prayer by watching and listening to those around them. Helping a baby make the sign of the cross might not register with their minds at such a young age, but it engrains within their hearts a new habit of grace, virtue, and love for God that will remain as an imprint on what they think and do as they begin to get older.

Another important step in child development is to teach a baby from a young age the name of Jesus and Mary, to show them pictures, to sing songs to them, to read from Scripture – so that God is a normal part of the lifeblood of their lives. Teaching a child the basics of the faith is like giving them the bricks to build the house (of their hearts); it is like the cells that form a person or the clay of a sculpture, the strokes of a painter's brush on a canvas, the notes in a musical arrangement. Teaching children the basic tenets of the faith from the youngest age will catapult them toward heaven. It will reflect every part of their lives and being as they grow into adulthood.

What you learn as a child stays with you forever. This is why it is important to teach the habit of prayer. Teaching children routine prayers (to always pray before meals, when they wake up and before they go to sleep, when they hear a siren or see someone upset or in trouble) will be like giving them strong foundations that they can fall back upon when life inevitably gets difficult. Routine prayer is like the hinges that keep them connected to God. And by teaching them to whisper a 'Hail Mary' when they feel stress or are worried is giving them the tools they need to endure anything that comes their way in life. It also reminds them regularly that they are not in control of life – God is – and this reminder helps them choose what is in their power (daily decisions that they encounter) according to the ways and will of God (who is ultimately in control of everything).

A child also learns right judgment from a young age. All of life is made up of decisions big and small. "Should I obey Mama?" "What color do I want to wear?" "Should I share my toys?" As a child is learning to make judgments in life, it is a great help to teach them right from the beginning to do so according to what God teaches is right. "Obedience is important." "Colors are not important in themselves." "Sharing is important."

One of the easiest ways to teach children right judgment is to teach them the rudiments of the faith through the catechism. Memorizing little phrases from the Baltimore Catechism is like giving their minds 'good wiring' – keeping their ways of thinking in conformity with Christ. Teaching Scripture does that as well. Both stories of virtuous people in the Bible as well as the teachings of Christ Himself give a roadmap for them to follow in their journey towards heaven. Stories of the lives of the saints also provide concrete models of holiness for children to follow. Children automatically mimic what they see and hear around them. And so, in addition to parents and other family members setting a good example to small children, teaching catechism and stories from the lives of the saints from a young age will strengthen them in the resolve to be good and holy children of God.

<u>Icons</u>

In addition to teaching catechism to children and illustrating the truths of Christ through Biblical stories, children are also formed by the arts. Images are so important for children. What a person looks at remains in his or her mind forever. And often small children without the ability to pay attention to long lessons about God are able to learn very quickly a similar lesson through simply looking at a picture or image of it. Icons are holy images –and the Eastern Church teaches that icons are such instruments of God's grace to reach the human soul that they are considered 'windows to heaven.' A child is never too young to begin to show such 'windows to heaven' in order to draw their heart to heavenly things. Not only can looking at holy images imprint goodness and God's love upon a child's heart, but such images naturally draw forth a desire in a child to imitate such beauty. Children love to color, draw, and paint – and so it can be very beneficial to a child's spiritual development to encourage 'holy art' – drawing, coloring, or painting holy things of God. The Holy Spirit is needed to do such 'holy art', and so by teaching this method to children you are in essence teaching them to cooperate with the Holy Spirit. And the Holy Spirit is Love, so you are teaching them to create 'in love' and 'for Love (God)' in imitation of our Creator.

Music

Music is another artistic form that can be used with the Holy Spirit to draw a child's soul into an atmosphere of the eternal. Music can be a conduit for prayer – and in itself a form of prayer. Music can be used from a child's very conception as a channel of grace. Parents who sing holy songs to their child in utero are teaching the child of their belovedness to God and teaching (even at this young age) the act of rejoicing. Children naturally love music, and filling this music with spiritually uplifting lyrics and the presence of prayerful love, you can very easily guide even a baby into the act of worship and praise of the Almighty, which brings with it joy.

Spiritual Direction

The French philosopher Blaise Pascal once said, "Le cœur a ses raisons que la raison ne connaît point," which in English means, **"The heart has its reasons that reason**

does not know." This is a quote that is very apropos to the section of this book about spiritual direction for children. This is because children, more than living from the mind, live from the heart. The first language that they learn to speak is the language of love – something beyond words – something that they speak with their hearts. And what is even more than that, the voice of God that guides a soul in their path of life back to Him in heaven is a voice that speaks not so much to the mind as to the heart.

The Catholic Catechism explains that:

> *"...the heart is the dwelling place where I am, where I live...it is our hidden center, beyond the grasp of our reason and of others; only the Spirit of God can fathom the human heart and know it fully. The heart is the place of decision, deeper than our psychic drives. It is the place of truth, where we choose life or death. It is the place of encounter, because as image of God we live in relation: it is the place of covenant." (2563)*

It also states:

> *"Whether prayer is expressed in words or gestures, it is the whole man who prays. But in naming the source of prayer, Scripture speaks sometimes of the soul or the spirit, but most often of the heart (more than a thous*

times.) According to Scripture, it is the heart that prays.
If our heart is far from God, the words of prayer are in
vain." (2562)

If a human heart is the sanctuary of God, beyond reason, only understood by Him, our Creator, then it is a place accessible for children of the youngest age to meet with God. It is not limited to the use of reason (which comes to them later on in life.) It is that place where even the smallest child in the womb of his or her mother can *'be still and know that I am God'* (Psalm 46:10).

The soul (heart) of a person 'knows' God – regardless of age. Deep within the sanctuary of the human heart each person has an innate connection with the Holy Spirit. And the Holy Spirit is living – is LIFE. Each person was not only created once by God, but every moment of every day they are being recreated by God. And He communicates to this beloved child of His through Love continually. A child must be taught to listen with the ears of the heart, to see with the eyes of the heart – to even think with the 'mind' of the heart – even (and especially) as they grow and mature into adults. God is ever fashioning them for Himself and in the life of Grace, and this primary relationship of a child with God should be nurtured as much as possible so that it bears forth the greatest fruit.

One way that God communicates and relates to a child (besides through simply the Presence of His Love) is by the spiritual gift of prophesy. This is a gift of mystical prayer – and children are powerful receptors of such communication with God. Their simplicity and purity of heart are clear reflectors of His voice. And so, it is powerful for children to learn as they grow how to 'stay little' in the arms of God, how to listen and see with their heart, and how to pay attention to His voice in their conscience that speaks to them and guides them. Mystical prayer is hidden prayer – and it is in the silence of a child's heart where God will most profoundly reveal who He created them to be – not only in a specific vocation in life – but even more so in the core soul of their being. It is here where He will infuse strength, beauty, light, grace, and love to radiate out from them to the world. For this reason, it is so important for children to cultivate their 'life of the heart' just as much as they cultivate physical, mental, and emotional milestones.

Matthew 11:25-26 *"At that time Jesus said in reply, "I give praise to you, Father, Lord of heaven and earth, for although you have hidden these things from the wise and the learned you have revealed them to the childlike. Yes, Father, such has been your gracious will."*

Listening to God

The Catechism of the Catholic Church says (quoting *Lumen Gentium*), *"Parents have the mission of teaching their children to pray and to discover their vocation as children of God."* (2226) It is important to teach children how to communicate with God – both how to speak and share their lives with Him, as well as how to listen to Him. God speaks differently to different souls. We are all unique, and God utilizes that individuality speaking to each human heart in the specific 'language' they can understand. Some people hear the voice of God directly, others find it clearly in Scripture, and others hear it in the lives of the saints, in homilies at Mass, in an image placed in their hearts or through music. Children are as unrepeatable as flowers and snowflakes – and so the way that God will relate to them will be just as numerous and particular to their own gifts, weaknesses, likes and dislikes. And because of this there is no one way to teach a child to listen to the voice of God in prayer. Yes, all children can be sure of God's voice speaking His will for them in Scripture, in the teachings of the Church, and in those placed in authority over them (most often parents and teachers). But above and beyond this, God has a very intimate relationship with each of their souls and there are special individual words He wants to speak directly to them. And yet you cannot tell them exactly how to listen to Him. Instead, you have to teach them to pray to the Holy Spirit and offer options and then allow God Himself to reveal Himself to their hearts.

Sometimes, I will take a child and simply suggest that they take a few minutes in silence and then either draw or write what comes to their mind. For some children, it is easier to prompt them with a question "What is God's Love to you?" or "What word do you think God is speaking to you?" or "What do you think God wants you to do when you grow up?" If the child doesn't draw or write the experience down himself, you can do it for him or her – and then keep these little prayer experiences together in a box or folder for him to go through again another day. You can read a Scripture story and then ask the child how he or she feels about it or what God is telling him or her in it. You will be amazed at how profound some of the answers will be –because they are answers straight from the Holy Spirit.

A beautiful example of the Lord's speaking directly to a child like this we see in the Old Testament story of young Samuel. As a boy sleeping in the Temple one night, he was awakened by the voice of the Lord calling to him, calling him by name: *"Samuel, Samuel."* The priest Eli instructed him to answer *'Speak, Lord, your servant is listening.'* And when Samuel did as he was instructed, the Lord began speaking to him as a prophet, using him as His Own mouthpiece for the people. What would keep the Lord from calling upon a child in our own day to do the same? But we must instruct our children to listen for Him and to respond – with faith, trust, openness, docility, and courage.

More important than to teach them about WHAT God says to them is to teach them THAT God loves them and speaks to them. By their being made aware of His constant presence in their lives, they will feel less lonely when sufferings happen, and they will more easily recognize His voice trying to guide them when they are tempted or meet a confusing situation. Most important is that children learn to lean upon a love relationship with God throughout the normal, daily activities of life. And then His Love – which is always creative and new – will find the perfect answers to their questions and needs.

It is important to note that most people receive a seed of their vocation (even if it is not understood in totality) as a child – usually at age 3 or 4 if you can teach them to listen to God at this point. This is because they have moved from a relationship of simply relating in love to God (as a baby does) into the realm of imagination, emotions, shapes, and colors. Before reason begins to block out that primary presence of God's Love speaking to their soul, He can show them a prophetic idea of His plans for their lives. And although not every child will know exactly his or her vocation at this age, God will begin to put clues as to what direction He wants him or her to follow. The child's parents can reinforce these experiences simply by praying for the Holy Spirit to expand them and by redirecting the child back to them when the world, with its glitter and gold, starts to attract him or her away from God.

Regular discussion with children about their experiences in prayer can also reiterate these experiences to the child's heart and help imprint them, confirming them in a way, and making them 'real' signposts for children to follow in life. For this reason, it is good to have the habit of sharing spiritual things with children through conversations – whether it be prayers, questions, opinions, etc. - it makes speaking about Godly things 'real' and 'firm' and 'practical' in their daily lives. By gathering the 'clues' about one's vocation that a child might receive at this little age (whether it be by writing them down or simply discussing them), the parent is naturally helping them discern in openness, honesty, and freedom the life that God created for them to follow.

Developing/Teaching Active Virtue

"Without confidence and love, there can be no true education. If you want to be loved...you must love yourselves, and make your children feel that you love them." –St. John **Bosco**

Another important topic to touch upon when reflecting on spiritual formation and direction of children is the concrete teaching of virtue. People often don't realize that children need to be taught virtue. Concupiscence takes root in all human hearts allowing people (beginning in childhood) to be tempted away from what is good and true and holy. Virtue is not something that comes easy – something acquired by simply floating down the river of grace. Instead, children must be taught how to seek out virtue – like stepping stones in a roaring river – and to exert their will to accomplish them, even when difficult. Children need things repeated to them over and over again in order to learn them. This is true of what they are told verbally as well as how they are taught to live. We are creatures of habit, and so children must be taught concretely how to develop virtuous habits in life.

And yet, what this quote from St. John Bosco emphasizes is the important point that children will only learn virtue when they find themselves in an atmosphere of love. So first and foremost in the development of virtue in the life of a child, the caretaker must ensure that the child is learning in an atmosphere of love. Once this connection of love is made, then the child will naturally want to follow the instructive words and actions regarding forming habits of virtue. After a love relationship is formed, then the adult needs to actively work at teaching the child to be virtuous and holy.

For example, from a young age a child needs to be taught to not be selfish – but instead to share. Whether it be food, their mom, or their favorite toy, children tend to be possessive and so a child must not only be told but also be shown what it means to share. The same is true of patience. Children want things 'now,' so little by little a parent must teach them to wait – whether it be for everyone to come to the table to start dinner or if it be patience with a younger sibling who absentmindedly knocked down their building made of blocks. In a similar way, children need to be taught temperance and moderation. For example, TV is not bad in moderation when used for good – so a child should be taught that they can enjoy a TV show for 30 minutes a day – in moderation – and then they need to put that aside and go outside to play. Children are taught modesty – not to run around in front of strangers or company naked. Children need to be taught obedience – even before they can speak, they understand what their parent means by 'yes' and 'no,' and they need to be taught the importance of respect of authority and obedience. Children also need to be taught kindness and generosity – doing good works for the poor – praying before they eat, etc. The list is endless – my point is simply that virtue is an act of the will, and these acts of the will can be taught in tiny bite size pieces from the youngest age. Most importantly, children must be taught that virtue is only holy when done in Love.

One practical way to do this in a family is to write out a 'virtue of the week' and hang it on the fridge. The family can discuss it at prayer time or during dinner together on Sunday. Maybe a Bible story or other creative way to ex-plain the virtue could be presented – with both of the parents clearly dictating what that virtue looks like in their everyday life – and what the family expectations regarding it are. Maybe at the family rosary in the evening they could pray together for that virtue – that they grow as a family in practicing it. This is just one example of a practical way to teach children the right way to live. But it is very important that parents don't just 'leave children to be as they are' – but instead as a good gardener would – actively work to cultivate virtue and goodness, right judgment, and love of God in the lives of their children.

Guardian Angels

"See that you do not despise one of these little ones, for I say to you that their angels in heaven always look upon the face of my heavenly Father." - Matthew 18:10

Besides all of the helps we have already listed that the Lord gives to those training children in holiness of life, I want to specifically mention the gift of guardian angels. God has assigned to each child a guardian angel to watch over him or her day and night and to not only keep him or her physically safe, but also to protect him or her spiritually and to bring his or her prayers to the throne of God – to help him or her grow in holiness. The gift of guardian angels will be more efficacious in the life of a child if he or she is taught about this holy presence always at his or her side and if he or she is taught to call upon the guardian angel as his or her best friend, a protector, a guide, and an encourager. The more that a child is aware of his or her guardian angel's being with him or her at all times, the more the child will be careful to correct his or her behavior, the more he or she will trust that his or her prayers are listened to, the more he or she will also grow to hear the voice of God speaking through his or her angel (maybe not audibly to his or her ears, but surely speaking silently to his or her heart.) Every morning and every evening, children should be taught to call upon these heavenly friends, especially with the 'Angel of God' prayer:

"Angels of God, our guardians dear;
to whom God's Love commits us here;
ever this day be at our sides;
to light and guard, to rule and guide. Amen."

Section Three

Apostolate of Children of the Cross

Children as Missionaries

Children as Contemplatives

Teaching Sacrifice

Children's Prayer

Children and the Evangelical Councils
(Poverty, Chastity and Obedience for
Children)

Setting Spiritual Goals

Prayers and Specifics about
'Children of the Cross' Prayer Groups

Chapter 8

The Apostolate of
The Children of the Cross

"Children of the Cross" is a Prayer Apostolate made up primarily of children dedicated to praying for priests and persecuted Christians. These little cenacles of prayerful Love meet on the Frist Friday of the Month to pray the Chaplet of Mercy, one decade of the Rosary, the Chaplet of Sorrows (if time allows), and spontaneous prayer of the children for priests and persecuted Christians all over the world. The children are invited and encouraged to bring with them to these prayer meetings pictures of any priests and persecuted Christians/communities that they want to specifically include in the prayer. We pray that this little, hidden Apostolate of childlike love may spread a perfume of grace throughout the world.

Children as Missionaries

When the Bible was translated into Latin, the word that Jesus used when sending out the disciples to preach the Gospel, was translated "*missionem*" meaning "act of sending" or "*mittere*," meaning "to send." "*Missionem*" was later translated into English as "missionary." Each Christian when baptized is anointed as 'priest, prophet and king'. And after they are baptized into the Body of Christ, they are 'sent out' as missionaries to the world – to witness even more than by their words, *by their lives* to the Truth of Jesus' Christ and His Teachings. All Christians – both old and young – are called to be 'missionary' in their everyday lives. This includes children. Before we talk about developing that missionary spirit in a child's life, let's review the Church's teaching on this missionary aspect and call of every Christian. The Catechism of the Catholic Church explains:

849 ***The missionary mandate.*** *"Having been divinely sent to the nations that she might be 'the universal sacrament of salvation,' the Church, in obedience to the command of her founder and because it is demanded by her own essential universality, strives to preach the Gospel to all men": "Go therefore and make disciples of all nations, baptizing them in the name of the Father and of the Son and of the Holy Spirit, teaching them to observe all that I have commanded you; and Lo, I am with you always, until the close of the age."*

850 The origin and purpose of mission. The Lord's missionary mandate is ultimately grounded in the eternal love of the Most Holy Trinity: "The Church on earth is by her nature missionary since, according to the plan of the Father, she has as her origin the mission of the Son and the Holy Spirit." The ultimate purpose of mission is none other than to make men share in the communion between the Father and the Son in their Spirit of love.

851 Missionary motivation. It is from God's love for all men that the Church in every age receives both the obligation and the vigor of her missionary dynamism, "for the love of Christ urges us on." Indeed, God "desires all men to be saved and to come to the knowledge of the truth"; that is, God wills the salvation of everyone through the knowledge of the truth. Salvation is found in the truth. Those who obey the prompting of the Spirit of truth are already on the way of salvation. But the Church, to whom this truth has been entrusted, must go out to meet their desire, so as to bring them the truth. Because she believes in God's universal plan of salvation, the Church must be missionary.

852 **Missionary paths.** *The Holy Spirit is the protagonist, "the principal agent of the whole of the Church's mission." It is he who leads the Church on her missionary paths. "This mission continues and, in the course of history, unfolds the mission of Christ, who was sent to evangelize the poor; so the Church, urged on by the Spirit of Christ, must walk the road Christ himself walked, a way of poverty and obedience, of service and self-sacrifice even to death, a death from which he* *emerged victorious by his resurrection." So it is that "the blood of martyrs is the seed of Christians."*

863 *The whole Church is apostolic, in that she remains, through the successors of St. Peter and the other apostles, in communion of faith and life with her origin: and in that she is "sent out" into the whole world.* <u>**All members of the Church share in this mission, though in various ways.**</u> *"The Christian vocation is, of its nature, a vocation to the apostolate as well." Indeed, we call an apostolate "every activity of the Mystical Body" that aims "to spread the Kingdom of Christ over all the earth."*

913 *"Thus, <u>**every person**</u>, through these gifts given to him (at Baptism), is at once the witness and the living instrument of the mission of the Church itself 'according to the measure of Christ's bestowal."' (Lumen Gentium 33, Eph 4:7)*

Some people might balk at the suggestion that children are called to be missionaries. And yet, to be made a child of God in Baptism and filled with the Light of Christ immediately transforms a child into a missionary (whether they are old enough to recognize it or not) – for they begin at that moment of Baptism to shine the Light of Jesus in the world, thus proclaiming His Love.

And although all people are called to a missionary work in the Church (to know one's faith, to live one's faith and to teach one's faith to those one encounters on a daily basis), sometimes children do this best of all. The simple humility of a child makes him or her automatically speak Truth, not looking at who might accept or reject it. And the purity of a child makes that proclamation a powerful instrument of the Holy Spirit to reach whoever he is speaking to. Scripture itself says:

"O LORD, our Lord, how awesome is your name through all the earth! I will sing of your majesty above the heavens <u>with the mouths of babes and infants</u>. You have established a bulwark against your foes, to silence enemy and avenger." (Psalm 8:2-3)

And

<u>"Out of the mouths of babes you have found perfect praise...</u>" (Matthew 21:16)

To be a missionary is to be a witness of Love – and this is done so easily by children since they innately love people. In this way a child is called to be a martyr as well – for a martyr is a 'witness' and the way that a little one lives his or her faith is a powerful witness in this world. Most children will not be called to be physical martyrs (those who shed their blood in witness to their faith in Christ), but some reading this book may be. All children need to be raised with such strong adherence to the Gospel (a strong attachment only able to be formed by one's intense love for Jesus Christ) that they would be willing to die for Him and their faith if tested in such a way. We have many examples of child saints who refused to deny Christ even when faced with death, and these little martyr saints should be held up to children as models for their own lives. Children should not just be taught to know and follow Jesus and His Church lukewarmly, but instead their fiery, passionate Love should forge their union with Him as strong as iron – and their Hope in the Life He promised us in Heaven should be the light that inspires them with courage when faced with death.

Even when children do not live in a place where their physical lives are threatened because of their faith, they must be raised with a 'martyr's heart' – a heart as strong in the teachings of the Church as the heart of a martyr. There are many temptations in the world today that can only be overcome by the fiercest and most courageous love and faithfulness. The interior martyrdom experienced by most Christians in the world today is no less difficult to embrace. Some children will be mocked for their faith, will lose a job later in life because they wouldn't morally agree to some-thing demanded of them, will be asked to 'go against the tide' in their social life, educational life, or even at times against others in the Church who live their faith more watered down. All children must be formed to have a 'martyr's heart,' to be a witness to Christ in the world.

When my 12 siblings and I were little, my Dad used to sit us down regularly for family meetings. At these meetings, he would teach us how everyone is watching us – whether we see it or not – and eventually in life what they see us do and how they hear us speak will all come back to us. He used to encourage us in living good and holy witnesses of our faith (and upholding respect of our family name) by how we behaved and with whom we chose to spend our time over the course of our lives.

Children are called to be missionaries in three ways: by their words, by their actions, and by their prayers. How a child speaks can teach others about Christ. First, this is done by always using good and holy language. Christians should never use bad language or talk in a way that is sinful – our words should reflect our relationship with Christ.

But even more than this, a child can be taught to be a missionary through his or her words in spreading the Gospel among relatives, neighbors, and friends. Telling other children (and sometimes adults) about their love for Jesus and what they understand of His teachings is a great way for children of any age to be missionary. Sometimes, this can be done in a conversation, but it also can be done in song – in music. Singing is a great way to bring others to

Christ – whether it be singing religious carols at a nursing home during Christmas or teaching a favorite song to a friend. Simply by a child's singing about Jesus he can spread His Light in the world.

Children are also called to be missionary by their actions – by living the Gospel. This can be taught to a child by encouraging him to be helpful and respectful to others or to share. This can be done hidden at home (by sharing a toy) or also as a public witness by helping a parent bring groceries to the poor. A child should be taught about how their actions speak.

Another way to teach a child to be missionary in their action is to teach them to be respectful of holy things – to kiss a crucifix or make the sign of the cross when passing a Church in the car or on a walk. Actions speak louder than words at times.

Lastly, a child is called to be missionary through prayer – and it is in this way that a child can be a missionary reaching people all over the world – in distant lands who speak different languages – simply by praying for them. A child should be taught the power of prayer. When they hear a siren, children should stop and pray for the police or paramedics and those who need help. A child should be taught as a first reaction to a difficult situation to pray – if they see a friend upset at school or if the child is afraid. And a child should never hesitate to ask those around him or her to join with him or her in prayer. He can be a missionary and reach an uncle who left the church, just by inviting him to pray with him before a meal. The power of a child's prayer is endless.

Children as Contemplatives (Hermits)

"What did Jesus say to you while you were praying?" I asked one of my little nieces after Mass one day. She answered, *"He said that my heart is just like yours, Aunt Mary. It's a cave where I meet with Him."* I was blown away. I had never described my heart as a cave to anyone, let alone this child. And although I lived as a hermit during this time of my life, I spoke more about hermitages than caves. Her answer was straight from the Holy Spirit.

Truly, every human heart is created as a 'cave' – a hidden place, out of the way, where a person can meet with God in solitude, silence, simplicity and prayer. Some children – through the grace of the Holy Spirit – will innately recognize this intimate place within their own hearts where they can meet with God. When I was a small child – maybe 1st or 2nd grade – I remember my older sister Cheryl taking me to our parish church one day when it was empty and quiet to take a few minutes to pray. When we left, she asked me what I prayed about or what God spoke to my heart. I said, *"Nothing. I was just 'being' with Him. We just sit together and 'be.'"* She was amazed by such a profound experience of contemplative prayer in a soul so small and she reassured me that this was very good, saying: *"Mary, that is called contemplative prayer. It's the highest form of prayer."* I remember that although I told her nothing, I felt guilty when she said that – like I must have described it wrong because there was no way I had a 'high form of prayer' in my little mind. But as an adult reflecting upon the experience, I realize that it is not that strange for the Holy Spirit to take a simple child so close to His Own Heart through such an experience. As an adult, I have often seen children of a very young age quickly swept up into a loving prayer of silent adoration with God.

Although some children might find this way of relating with God on their own, there are ways that you can encourage the contemplative life in a child. You can explain to them that their heart is a 'cell', a 'cloister', a 'cave,' or a 'garden' within them. You can teach children about keeping one's heart 'silent' before God – listening for Him. You can teach them about worship and adoration of God – putting forth the example of the poor shepherds in Bethlehem – and from this authentic stance of adoration, praise, and worship God can lead them quickly and easily deep into union with Him.

Eucharistic adoration is a wonderful atmosphere where a child can learn to relate to God in a contemplative way. It is naturally silent there – and the simple focus of the Eucharistic Bread – along with superabundant amounts of grace can quickly unite a child's heart in not only the 'prayer of the quiet' but actual union with God. And a child's natural purity and humility makes this happen very quickly. The greatest strides that can be made in a child's spiritual life will take place in front of the Eucharistic Lord. And there is no greater honor a child could give to God than adoration of His Presence, Goodness, and Love.

As a child is taught contemplative prayer, it is good to help guide him or her in this time to listen to God – and a spiritually perceptive adult will be able to see, even at an early age, clues about that child's vocation. This time of adoration can help a child discern in openness and freedom what path to take in life in order to grow closest with God.

I used to lead 'Missionary Hermit' retreats for small children and at first glance some may question how (or if) it is possible for a child to live like a hermit. But my own hermit vocation was born in my heart as a child. My little brother and I created a special secret dark place behind the basement stairs where we would go with a lantern to read the Bible. We created two other similar spots in the woods outdoors and we would withdraw there to pretend we lived in nature and to pray. I didn't really know the word 'hermit' at that age, but I was pretending to be exactly what a hermit is.

Later on in life when I was questioned by children as to my vocation as a hermit, I would explain the 'pillars' of silence and solitude, prayer and fasting, poverty, chastity, and obedience. When children said they wanted to live like me – I simply adapted these things to their vocation and state of life (being that of a child). People might think that the word 'hermit' is wrong for a child to live, and yet when you realize how these pillars of the eremitical life can be adapted to paths of virtue for a child's footsteps, it becomes obvious how easily a child can imitate a hermit in their quest for sanctity.

Prayer can easily be taught to a child. We have already talked about that at length. Fasting (the idea of offering things up in sacrifice) can also be taught to a child. St. Therese of Lisieux was given 'sacrifice beads' by her sisters as a child where she would count the sacrifices that she would make for the Lord. Total silence and solitude are not appropriate for a child's learning language and proper human relationships. But the idea of taking some time of the day (even 5 minutes) to withdraw to be alone and quiet with God is something that would benefit all children. Also, in a world where noise is everywhere, it would be a great blessing to a child to be taught to turn off the phone, the TV, the internet, and music – and to just be in quiet with God as they play. It is also easy (and important) to teach children poverty (the idea of not being possessive or selfish), chastity (modesty and purity of one's body and heart can be taught from a very early age) and, of course, obedience – which is important to a child's personal development. I will touch on these last three things (poverty, chastity, and obedience) in the life of a child in a separate section below.

One last thing that I always included in my 'missionary hermit retreats' with children was the gift of doing sacred art (specifically painting icons). This is a 'work' that hermits for centuries have embraced. Painting sacred images comes about best when the artist first takes a time for prayer, fasting, in silence and solitude – and inviting the Divine Hand of the Father to work with them in what they create. Lighting a blessed candle or playing holy chant music can create an atmosphere of prayer where the child more naturally be docile to the Holy Spirit's inspiration and guidance as they work. Magnificent images with profound spiritual meaning can be painted by a child when they are instructed how to work best with the Holy Spirit. And these images go way beyond the paper, the canvas, or the wood they paint – these images (that they create in union with the Holy Spirit) are forever etched simultaneously on their minds and hearts.

<u>Children's Prayer</u>

A child's prayer is oftentimes very simple, but this makes it profound. St Therese of Lisieux (with her spirituality of littleness) used to describe prayer thus: **"For me, prayer is a surge of the heart; it is a simple look turned**

toward heaven, it is a cry of recognition and of love, embracing both trial and joy." This is something very accessible even to the smallest babies (looking towards heaven, a cry of love). *The Catechism of the Catholic Church* further explains prayer in such a way that those who are smallest – with the humblest of hearts – are most able to pray well. It says:

> <u>**2559**</u> *"Prayer is the raising of one's mind and heart to God or the requesting of good things from God." (St. John Damascene) But when we pray, do we speak from the height of our pride and will, or "out of the depths" of a humble and contrite heart? (Ps 130:1) He who humbles himself will be exalted; (Lk 18:9-14) humility is the foundation of prayer, Only when we humbly acknowledge that "we do not know how to pray as we ought," (Rom 8:26) are we ready to receive freely the gift of prayer. "Man is a beggar before God." (St. Augustine)*

If humility is the foundation of prayer, then even deep prayer is very accessible to the smallest of children (for they have a natural humility, so to say). Even if the simplest of words can be used in speaking with God (and children should be encouraged to speak with God simply from their heart), it is also very helpful for children to learn rote prayers (the Rosary, Chaplet of Divine Mercy, prayers before meals and before bed and the Angel of God prayer).

In times of crisis in life (or in the midst of struggles and sufferings), sometimes all we can muster is to repeat a prayer that we learned as a child. When this happens, the prayer carries us. In this regard, it is also a great grace to teach children prayers in the form of songs. These can be praise songs that are original or simple prayers and bible verses put to music. In this way, they more easily remember them, and their hearts are filled with joy as they repeat them (singing). Plus, as St. Augustine is noted as saying, *"One who sings, prays twice."*

It is also a great grace to teach children meditation. Children naturally use their imaginations, and they love stories, so reading a child a bible story and teaching them how to meditate on it (which is basically prayerfully thinking about the story) is a way to really help their heart grow in their knowledge and love of God. One can ask a child how a story makes them feel, which character they would like to be, or what God is trying to teach them in it.

Teaching Children to Sacrifice (and the Idea of Fasting)

Children shouldn't 'fast' so to say – as their little bodies are growing, they need to consume proper nutrition. Yet children can (and should) be taught the idea of sacrifice. This can be giving up a dessert or watching TV, or it can be doing a chore they do not particularly like, etc. The idea of sacrificing what one enjoys in order to offer it as a prayer is salutary for any soul (young or old). The universe does not revolve around any of us. God is the center of the universe. And the sooner we learn to not be selfish, greedy, indulgent, etc., the better the world around us will be and the happier we will be in our hearts as well.

I mentioned before how children should be taught to cultivate virtue – and this includes the idea of sacrificing what one wants in order to make another person happy (maybe giving up a cherished toy to a younger sibling). But it's not only sacrificing for another person that should be taught to our youngsters, but also the idea of sacrifice in and of itself as a gift (of prayerful love) to God. Sacrifice has power because it empties us of something in order to make room for God to have more space in us to fill and work through. This is why Our Lady emphasized so greatly the necessity of making acts of sacrifice to Bernadette in Lourdes and the three children in Fatima. If a child learns the spirit of sacrifice when young, he will easily grow into the idea of fasting from food and other things when he is older. This will strengthen his will, which in turn helps him in other moral areas of his life – for with a strong will adhering to God and His ways, one easily overcomes temptations to vice and sin.

Children and The Virtues of Poverty, Chastity and Obedience

Poverty – Teaching the Simple Idea of Generosity and Sharing

The evangelical counsel of poverty is different from physical destitution. The church would never ask for the Christian to be destitute – it is required for justice's sake that we help all people to have the necessary food, shelter, clothing, and medical care to be healthy citizens of society. Yet, there is a real gift (and grace) of poverty that is asked of the Christian as they seek after Christ. Jesus Himself said, *"Blessed are the poor in spirit, for theirs is the Kingdom of Heaven."* (Mt 5:3) To be 'poor in spirit' means more than just being humble and empty of oneself. It also means that a person should try to embrace a simple and generous stance of heart according to their state in life.

Children can easily be taught the root virtues of generosity and sharing – selflessness – that are the core behind the call to a life of poverty for the Lord. God looks at the heart of a person more than anything else, and teaching children to share, to forget themselves, to be generous in thought, word and action, forms them into the image of our poor Savior Who was born in a stable and Who died naked on a Cross.

Chastity – cultivating purity of heart

Chastity is modesty and purity. *"Blessed are the pure of heart, for they shall see God."* (Mt. 5:8) Children innately are pure, and yet they must be taught modesty so that as they grow they naturally preserve their purity. Chastity or purity of heart is not just how one acts. It is also how one dresses (teaching a little child not to run around naked in front of company, for example). It is how one speaks (not allowing children to use profanity). It is what one looks at and listens to (making sure that TV programs they see and radio songs they hear are appropriate and not sexually insinuating). Purity is not in itself the absence of sin, but the presence of God. The more united one is with God, the more purity that soul will radiate in the world. And so, the best way to teach purity of heart is to bring a child into contact with the purity of God. In Eucharistic Adoration, a child sees the whiteness of Jesus in the Bread, hears His silence, apprehends His humility and docility – and these things are graces that infiltrate a child's heart, soul, and senses while in His presence and naturally encourages purity (and chaste modesty) in all that a child says and does.

Obedience

Every person must obey. They must obey God (whether they like it or not, there are eternal consequences to disobeying God). They must obey just laws. They must obey bosses at work and teachers at school. They must obey most adults when they are young and most obviously their parents, grandparents, aunts, uncles, older siblings when they are babysitting, and other guardians and caretakers. Obedience is part of life.

But there is obedience that frees us to be happy – this is what happens when we obey someone who demands something of us for our own good. Parents hopefully are always like this to their child – but even when they sin, God's rules are always perfect and something that grants a deep everlasting joy to those who follow Him. God places His Own voice deep within the heart and soul of every person – it is the voice of their conscience. This voice is like a roadmap guiding each child (when it is properly formed) on the best path to heaven. The goal of this voice is to take a soul to eternal happiness with God. Obedience to one's own conscience is a must if one wants to find peace and contentment. Even real joy.

A child learns obedience to God by practicing obedience to parents, grandparents, and caregivers. This obedience begins when they are very little in a spontaneous way – when they are told something they follow what Love is speaking to them. Yet as defiance begins to creep into a child's world as a temptation, a parent who doesn't insist on obedience is only doing something detrimental to their child's development. By teaching a child to obey (especially when they might not particularly want to) – and doing so in a strong, yet loving manner – a parent is teaching the child a tool that they will need for all their life. Jesus was *"obedient unto death, even death on a cross"* (Phil 2:8), and the life of a Christian following His footsteps will demand the same thing. A parent is doing a great good for a child in teaching him to obey in love what those in authority over him ask of him.

Spiritual Goals for Children

Here at the end, I want to encourage those who take care of and form children spiritually to help children grow in their life of virtue and love day by day. Like all things in life, if you aren't growing and going forward, you are usually decaying or going backwards. And so, we want to always be growing in Love – both of God and of our neighbor. That can be done by little steps – little changes and corrections and encouragements given daily and consistently. It is a great gift to a child to be taught how to set spiritual goals for life and then to be helped in achieving them. It might be the goal of learning a prayer or saying it daily; it might be the goal of going to confession once a month or sacrificing something they enjoy (ice cream) to give the money to the poor; it might be the goal of being patient or not talking back. But by concretely helping a child identify spiritual goals, it encourages growth and makes the child so excited and proud each time they achieve them.

Chapter 9

The Apostolate of the
Children of the Cross Prayer Groups

Practical about the prayer groups

The **Children of the Cross** Apostolate is a prayer apostolate for children (and adults with childlike hearts) who gather together to pray for priests and persecuted Christians. Ideally, the group meets the First Friday of the month, although in some places it is necessary to meet at another time or more often than just once a month. Children are encouraged to bring pictures of priests and those persecuted Christian communities that they want to specifically pray for – although their prayer encompasses the whole world.

Children are simple, and simplicity reaches straight into the Heart of God, and so these meetings do not need to be complicated. I encourage the group gathering to pray a rosary, a Chaplet of Divine Mercy or a Chaplet of Our Lady of Sorrows for priests and persecuted Christians. A short time of spontaneous prayer can be added. Those leading the groups could add any Christian prayers that the Holy Spirit places on their hearts – prayers to the angels and litanies, for example. There are many examples of prayers that could be used at these meetings in my Rosary Prayer Book, **Mornings with Mary,** published by *En Route Books and Media*. In the Chapter for Thursdays there are particularly several powerful prayers listed for priests.as well.

It is beneficial for children to pray in front of the Eucharist, but that is not always possible. If the group is gathering in a home or Church hall, it would be helpful for the children to have an icon of Jesus, a blessed candle and crucifix, or other holy objects to center their attention as they gather in prayer.

We ask that these groups briefly pray for each other as well. The groups can also share photos of the various groups praying (they are posted on my website: www.marykloskafiat.com) As children gather together remembering and supporting one another in love, their faith and trust in God (and the power of their prayer which unites them together) will also grow.

"My little children, your hearts are small, but prayer stretches them and makes them capable of loving God. Through prayer we receive a foretaste of heaven and something of paradise comes down upon us. Prayer never leaves us without sweetness. It is honey that flows into the souls and makes all things sweet. When we pray properly, sorrows disappear like snow before the sun." - Saint John Vianney

"May the Child Jesus be the Star that guides you through the desert of your present life." –St. Padre Pio

About Mary Kloska's Vocation

Mary Kloska is from Elkhart, Indiana. She was raised in a huge Polish family (12 brothers and sisters) along with a lot of foster babies and other needy people in and out of the house. She presently has 70+ nieces and nephews. She has lived a very unique life.

Upon graduating from Notre Dame in 1999 she spent almost 20 years in the missions serving the poor (including orphanages) as well as praying as a consecrated hermit all over the world – Siberia, Nigeria, Tanzania, South Africa, Philippines, Mexico, the Holy Land and all over Europe as well.

Although Mary spent a lot of time away in silence praying, ironically, she loves children and is very fun and outgoing when it comes to serving young adults, as well as the little ones. She also spent her time in the missions giving retreats, doing simple catechesis, leading prayer groups, giving spiritual direction, helping in deliverance, changing diapers, feeding babies and cleaning floors. After spending intense time serving in a mission she would withdraw for periods of 'retreat' as a hermit (including three years as an official diocesan hermit with vows under a Bishop.)

The last few years, Mary has spent as a full-time nanny to infant triplets, twins and several large families. She speaks many languages (poorly) and enjoys playing guitar, painting icons, baking, gardening, reading, writing and simply filling in where there is the greatest need in the Church. Her WCAT Radio program, "The Heart of Fiat Crucified Love," may be found on WCAT Radio, online at https://wcatradio.com/heartoffiatcrucifiedlove/

For more information about Mary Kloska's vocation, books, icons (Artist Shop), music, podcasts, prayer ministry or to become a monthly donor to support her missionary work, please see:

www.marykloskafiat.com

Blog: http://fiatlove.blogspot.com

Books:

The Holiness of Womanhood:
https://enroutebooksandmedia.com/holinessofwomanhood

Out of the Darkness:
https://enroutebooksandmedia.com/outofthedarkness/

In Our Lady's Shadow:
The Spirituality of Praying for Priests:
https://enroutebooksandmedia.com/shadow/

A Heart Frozen in the Wilderness: Reflections of a Siberian Missionary:
https://enroutebooksandmedia.com/frozen/
Mornings With Mary: A Rosary Prayer Book:
https://enroutebooksandmedia.com/morningswithmary/

La Santidad de La Mujer:
https://enroutebooksandmedia.com/lasantidaddelamujer/

Swietosc Kobiecosci:
https://enroutebooksandmedia.com/swietosckobiecosci/

Z Ciemnosci:
Z ciemności… | En Route Books and Media

Fuera de las Tinieblas:
https://enroutebooksandmedia.com/fueradelastinieblas/

Radio
Podcasts: https://wcatradio.com/heartoffiatcrucifiedlove/

YouTube VIDEO Podcasts
Playlist: http://www.tinyurl.com/marykloska

Artist Shop (Icon prints and other items for sale): http://marykloskafiat.threadless.com

Music CD "FIAT" is also available on all music platforms.

Patreon: www.patreon.com/marykloskafiat

Made in the USA
Middletown, DE
03 December 2021

53543239R00106